Collecting
ANTIQUE LINENS, LACE, & NEEDLEWORK

Collecting ANTIQUE LINENS *Lace &* NEEDLEWORK

FRANCES JOHNSON

WALLACE-HOMESTEAD
BOOK COMPANY
Radnor, Pennsylvania

To Kim
with Love

Copyright © 1991 by Frances Johnson

All Rights Reserved
Published in Radnor, Pennsylvania 19089, by Wallace-Homestead,
a division of Chilton Book Company

No part of this book may be reproduced, transmitted or stored
in any form or by any means, electronic or mechanical,
without prior written permission from the publisher

Designed by Anthony Jacobson
Manufactured in the United States of America

Library of Congress Cataloging in Publication Data
Johnson, Frances.
    Collecting antique linens, lace, and needlework / Frances Johnson.
        p. cm.
    Includes bibliographical references and index.
    ISBN 0-87069-634-3 (hc)   ISBN 0-87069-633-5 (pb)
    1. Household linens—Collectors and collecting.   2. Lace and lace
making—Collectors and collecting.   3. Needlework—Collectors and
collecting.   I. Title.
NK8904.J64   1991   91-16703
746′.075—dc20   CIP

    2   3   4   5   6   7   8   9   0   0   9   8   7   6   5   4

Contents

Foreword

I've always been drawn to old needlework. I search it out at garage sales, flea markets, and antiques shops. I appreciate the time and talent that goes into each piece and wonder about the person who made it, when it was accomplished, why it was created, and if its price tag actually reflects its value. I'm particular about what I buy and add to my collections.

Having been a member of an embroiderers' guild for more than twenty years, I've learned every type of needlework invented. No wonder I feel there should be more recognition for artists who work with needles. *Collecting Antique Linens, Lace, and Needlework* accomplishes this by making the reader more aware and respectful of the needle arts.

Arranged conveniently by needlework technique, Frances Johnson explains the fasci-nating origins, histories, and ways of identi-fying the pieces in our collections or those we are considering for purchase. And if you aren't one to hide your old needlework in a trunk or file it away museumlike, she also offers tips on how to use those old collectibles in new ways.

Another chapter explains how old pieces were cared for when first stitched and how to revitalize and take care of those pieces today.

Whether you are an experienced collector or a beginner; whether you buy needlework or needlework tools for an investment, beauty, history, or just for fun, you'll need the price guide. *Collecting Antique Linens, Lace, and Needlework* shows us not just the monetary values, however. It reveals the ways in which needlework enriches our lives.

—Jackie Dodson

Introduction

This book will hopefully help both the beginning and the advanced collector more easily recognize all types of old needlework and household linens. It is not always easy to make proper identification of some pieces unless we have a working knowledge of our ancestor's lifestyle. Most of the linens found today were made during the Victorian era, a time when everything was done on a grand scale. It was a time of ostentatious houses, furnishings, and living. Even the less affluent tried to copy the very rich. They couldn't entertain on the same grand scale, but they could make the same fancy household linens.

Household linens were essential if they were to maintain this stately lifestyle. Therefore, the ladies who didn't work outside the home (and that was the great majority of them) worked long hours making heavily decorated linens. They didn't have television, movies, or even radios, so they had few distractions other than caring for their families and entertaining. Entertaining was the frosting on the cake as it gave them an opportunity to show off the many household linens they continued to make.

For a decade or so into this century, the earlier linens were packed away in trunks and chests. Women continued to make some pieces, but they were not nearly as elaborate as those done by their mothers and grandmothers.

Then a decade or so ago those old linens that had been packed away began to be rediscovered. It is almost impossible now to look through a magazine devoted to decorating the home and not see dozens of ways to use old linens in modern homes. Their popularity has grown until it is almost impossible to find an antiques show, shop, or mall that doesn't have a wide variety available.

Recently, conversations with various antiques dealers seem to confirm the fact that old household linens, and some that aren't so old, are fast becoming the "in" collectible or antique. In fact, one mall owner said that linens were his bestsellers. This is probably true because malls offer such a wide variety of linens, making it easy to find nearly anything one wants.

As with all antiques, we tend to collect things that are most familiar to us, things we remember from grandmother's house. This applies to household linens as well as other antiques. It is quite noteworthy that younger collectors prefer the colored embroidery and crocheting made by their grandmothers, while the older collectors still search for the white on white—the kind made by *their* grandmothers.

Price is probably another factor in the rising popularity of needlework. It is still possible to find lovely pieces for less than $10; many can be found for less than $5. Pillow cases, especially linen (fabric) ones, are extremely scarce and when found often will have prices ranging from $30 for the plainer ones to as much as $75 or more for the ornately embroidered ones with wide crocheted or knitted edging. Then there are the towels and splashers that were made by the thousands to be used on washstands *before* bathrooms became a reality in many areas. These towels are still plentiful

1

and can be found for under $5 for the plainer ones to as much as $20 for the monogrammed versions with wide crocheted or tatted edging.

The wise collector will search for needlework pieces that have recently been laundered. By the same token she will avoid pieces with yellow or brown places. These indicate the pieces have lain folded the same way for long periods of time. Even if she can remove the spots or discoloration, there is still the possibility the fabric has been damaged and holes will begin to appear. This is especially true of pieces that have been folded the same way for years. The pressure on the folds has a tendency to weaken the threads, therefore the fabric will split along the folds. Try to fold your own linens a different way when they are laundered as this will help avoid that problem.

The best advice we can give beginning collectors is to examine each piece carefully before buying it. It may be neatly folded and beautifully packaged, but don't buy it unless you have checked it carefully for small holes that have been caused by wear and tear or by washing in strong solutions.

If the price is right, one might be wise to buy a damaged piece if the edging is of the best quality. In most cases the edging can be removed and put on a better piece that has no edging. Where there is only a small damaged place, it is often very easy to repair it, especially if the price is low and the quality of the workmanship is excellent.

CHAPTER 1

A Brief History of Antique Linens, Lace, and Needlework

The dictionary describes embroidery as the art or work of ornamenting fabric with needlework. This is such a simple way to describe some of the exquisite pieces of needlework— some that would and could compete with the most renowned paintings in the world. Like the paintings, the needlework was created with little more than the genius of a man or a woman. While the great paintings were done with only a brush, palette, and some paints, the embroideries were created just as simply with only a needle, thread, and sometimes a thimble.

The art of embroidery is as old as the growing of fibers, the spinning of yarn, and the weaving of fabrics. The first weavings were quite plain and rather crude, but they were something to satisfy the cravings of people who wanted their garments to have a personal touch—something different than that worn by their neighbors.

Originally embroidery was used only on the borders of garments; later it would be used exclusively on church linens and vestments, and finally on everything from clothing to household linens.

A type of embroidery was known and practiced by the Greeks centuries before the birth of Christ. At the time they used a chain stitch that could be called the first or original embroidery stitch. This same stitch still was being used by both the Romans and Byzantines several centuries later along with some other stitches they had created. This early embroidery was certainly not outstanding—in fact, it was rather plain and drab. It was not until the eleventh century that any really fine specimens began to be made. At that time most of the fine embroideries were being done in the convents and would be used in the churches.

It was about this same time that heraldry entered into the embroider's designs as they began to make military as well as sacred items. Previously, the work had consisted mainly of sacred events and personages because the work was to be used exclusively in churches.

Those who have thoroughly studied the old embroideries have noticed a great change in the work done between the eleventh and fifteenth centuries. A mingling of ideas from other countries shows how travel and the customs of others affected even the work of the closeted embroiderer. The work of this period was done with a finer and more elaborate stitch than had been previously used. Now they were combining shiny, silken threads with gold and silver ones, especially on the sumptuous vestments.

The designs and ornamentations usually had either a symbolic meaning or told a story. The latter has been most useful in tracing some of the history that otherwise would have been lost. Many of these early pieces traced battles and movements of troops as well as what loosely could be called the "current events" of that period. In fact, one of the oldest pieces of embroidery depicts many of the different events in the Norman Conquest of England. The drawings of the figures that were later embroidered look as if they had been done by a small child—and a not-very-talented child at that. The figures were certainly not in proportion with the balance of the work. The action was well suggested in this piece although the accuracy of the exact details is somewhat questionable.

During the twelfth and thirteenth centuries the convents of England became the homes of the most skilled embroiderers in the world. Not only did the nuns excel in needlework, but they also taught anyone who was willing to come in by the day and work on the embroideries. Homeless girls were given a home and taught to become expert needlewomen by the nuns. This group of embroiderers became renowned for their ecclesiastical embroidery.

A blue satin chasuble (the sleeveless outer vestment worn by the priest at Mass) that was made by this group has been described by Alan S. Cole in a 1900 issue of *Home Needlework Magazine* as "figured with heraldic animals, griffins, and lions amidst gracefully twining branches and stems embroidered principally of gold thread with short and regular stitches so as to give the surface of the gold forms a sort of diapered effect." It also was said that the termination of the leaves, the scrolling stems, the claws of the beasts, the wings of the griffins, and parts of the other figures were wrought in colored silks in fine chain stitch. The back of the chasuble was divided into four panels, each containing a representation of the crucifixion. The first showed the Virgin Mary on the throne, the second featured the figure of Saint Peter with two keys, the third was of Saint Paul with a sword, and the last presented the stoning of Saint Stephen. All panels were done in fine embroidery.

One of the copes, those capelike vestments worn by the priest, made during this period has been described as the most remarkable specimen of *opus anglicum* that has ever existed. Biblical figures worked on the cope begin with the Virgin Mary and baby Jesus, and are followed by David and Solomon, then Jesse, and to the left of these are figures representing Jacob, Eliachim, Thares, Abraham, and Abias while on the right are figures to represent Isaiah, Moses, Zorobabel, and Jeremiah. The foundation of the cope was made entirely of canvas, but the canvas was

Blue satin chasuble from an old picture.

completely concealed by the silk and gold embroidery. Mention is again made of the chain stitch as it was used extensively on the cope.

From all indications the English embroiderers were surpassed during the fifteenth and sixteenth centuries by the Flemish embroiderers, who began to use a great deal of gold thread laid on with a "couching stitch" that held the gold thread in place. This is the first record found of that stitch, therefore it is unknown whether the Flemish embroiderers created it or simply gained recognition for using it extravagantly. Like the English, the Flemish embroiderers, along with their students, worked in the convents, and the majority of their work still was done on church hangings and vestments. Their embroidery was so fine it often was compared to the Flemish tapestries of that era, those using religious, mythical, and historical themes.

The lion on this seat cover often was used on chasubles and copes as well.

Needlepoint seat covers often were used on chairs in and around the altar in later years.

By the sixteenth and seventeenth centuries Italy and France had joined the others in trying to compete for the best embroidery on the market. It was beginning to be sold to those who could afford it, and the demand was growing rapidly. No longer was it being used simply for church hangings and vestments, now it was beginning to be used on clothing again (but on a much larger scale), as well as on household linens. It was about this time that the use of figures began to be phased out and the use of flowers, plants, and geometric designs became more popular. Many of the embroidery designs used during that period appear to have been copied from the designs on buildings or those on metalwork. In some cases they seem to have been copied from the designs woven into the silk fabrics. No doubt many of the designs were the work of the embroiderer herself, as she was finally free to create and embroider her own design.

Several changes took place in the sixteenth and seventeenth centuries. The use of heavily embroidered velvet bed hangings became fashionable for those who could afford them. Embroidery was beginning to appear on doublets (tight-fitting jackets worn by the men during that period), on pockets, and on trunk hose (baggy pants that reached halfway to the

Animals in some of the church needlepoint are related to mythical and Biblical stories.

knees). Appliqué began to appear along with the embroidery during this period. Appliqué hasn't varied too much since then although it may be a little more refined today.

The piece to be appliquéd then was apparently cut out of silk, satin, or gold or silver fabric and then sewed on the background. Pieces of gimp or cord were sewed around the edges to give both a sharper outline and to protect the edges. Today the edges of the piece being appliquéd are turned under and whipped to the background. It can be left that way or it can be outlined with a blanket stitch. Early historians suggested that appliqué work was much better suited to upholstery for furniture than for clothing.

The first embroidery done in America was done by Dame Brewster, the wife of Elder Brewster, who played such an important part in the settling of Plymouth Plantation in Massachusetts. She made a picture of the English port of Plymouth, the port from which they

had sailed only a few months before; and it was done in elaborate embroidery, not the simple stitches used in the samplers. She embroidered the picture while living aboard the *Mayflower* as she and the other wives waited for the men to build homes or find some kind of shelter. The first American sampler was made by Loara Standish, a daughter of Miles Standish and his second wife, Barbara.

Embroidery in the New World continued from its beginnings on board the *Mayflower*. In the rural areas and on the farms it would be quite a while before the women had time to do much fancy embroidery. They first had to prepare and spin the thread that would be woven into fabric for their clothing and household linens. Whenever they had a little spare time, they might add a few decorative stitches. They loved fine needlework, so it was only a matter of time until they began to do lots of embroidery in their spare time. They realized the value of needlework, not only as a form of

Pieces of elaborately embroidered vestments are used to make pillows after they are discarded.

decoration for clothing and household linens but also as a very inexpensive yet rewarding pastime.

It was customary to teach young girls various embroidery stitches, and the custom continued in the New World. Although the chain stitch was the first stitch known to have been used, young girls in America started their training with the cross-stitch, as witnessed by the many samplers still to be found.

Once the child had mastered the various stitches used at that time, she was allowed to begin making linens for use in the home. Mastering those stitches could be a real chore for both the mother and the daughter judging by the reports that Rachel Jackson, wife of Andrew Jackson, had to rip out her stitches more than once to satisfy the demands of her mother. As the child grew into a young lady and her skills progressed, she began making fine linens for her dower or marriage chest. For a century or so after this country was settled, it was still the custom for each young girl to

spend much of her spare time embroidering linens for her dower chest. These linens would be used in her own home after she was married—and married she would be, even if her father had to increase the monetary dowry, for in those day it was a fate worse than death for a girl not to be married by the time she was eighteen years of age. Many married at the tender age of fourteen or fifteen.

Although the girls who lived in the cities filled a dower or hope chest like their country cousins, their lives were much easier. In the first place most of the people who settled in the towns and cities were originally from well-to-do families in the old country. The women were accustomed to an easier life than that faced by the wives of the early farmers and those who migrated westward. The ladies and girls in the cities already had been taught the fine art of needlework and they continued to practice it here. In New England Indian women often were hired as servants. Since they were accustomed to doing most of the work in

Crocheted altar cloth from a country church.

Many altar cloths stressed the fact that one must suffer before entering heaven.

the fields or gardens, they thought the new-comers were extremely lazy when they pre-ferred doing needlework to growing foods.

Although a few men are known to have become excellent needleworkers, it was and still is considered woman's work. Apparently, plying the needle is better suited to her temper-ament as she is supposed to have a lighter touch than a man, a very necessary element in needlework.

It is safe to say that in simple terms em-broidery could best be described as the art of creating scenes by using floral, geometric, and figure designs in various colors of thread on materials of assorted types. Although the exact origins of embroidery have never been found, old records show that somewhere in that dark, distant past it was called *phrygium* or *phrygian* work, and the embroiderers themselves were called *phrygios,* while the design only made in gold and silver at that time was called *auriphrygium.*

But as the art spread, the name changed according to the country where it was done. In Latin it was known as *brustus* or *aurobrus* but became *broderie* when it reached France. In England it was called embroidery, the same name that still is used by all English-speaking countries.

Chances that the average collector ever will find one of the old pieces of embroidery, one done with gold or silver thread, are practi-cally nil. But there are some excellent pieces available that have been made within the past century, and some are even older. Many of these pieces also were used in the churches. The beautiful embroidered vestments of the priests, particularly those in white, are well worth collecting as they can be used to enhance modern-day clothing and household linens. The heavily embroidered altar cloths make excellent pillow covers when they are no longer used in the church. Many of the old country churches had crocheted altar cloths, usually with a warning motto, such as "No Cross, No Crown." These can be used as pillow covers, or they can be framed over a black velvet back-ground.

CHAPTER 2
An Encyclopedia of Stitches

When used to describe embroidery, the term "stitches" should convey a completely different meaning than when the same word is used in connection with ordinary hand sewing. In the latter case the object is to hide the stitch as much as possible to make the work prettier; in embroidery the opposite is true, for without the fancy stitches there is no beauty. It is true that the relationship of stitches to embroidery has been compared to the relationship of notes to music (early embroiderers saw it), but embroidery is an art form all its own. It is not an imitation of any other form of expression.

The following list of stitches—some slight variations of old stitches that were given provocative names to intrigue new needleworkers—is not complete, but it will help collectors of old clothing and household linens recognize the various stitches used. It also could help a beginning embroiderer master the different stitches.

The *basket couching stitch* is one of the *most*

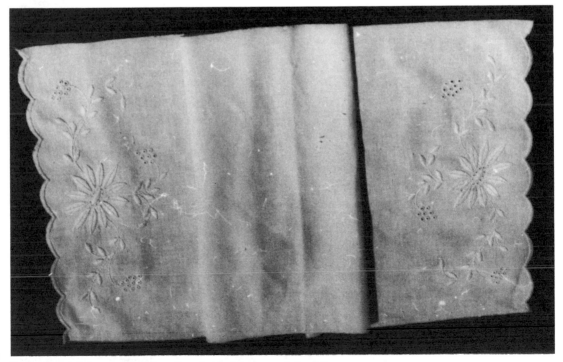

Embroidered dresser scarf with scallops finished in buttonhole stitch.

9

difficult stitches until you master the correct procedure. Over-and-under basket couching or stitching is worked over the cords that are first sewn to the fabric with a small hidden stitch. Silk embroidery thread is then worked over and under the cords, two at a time, making a basket weave effect.

Beading stitch is simply a variation of the old chain stitch. The chain loop is worked at a decided right angle over the thread laid on the outline. It gives the effect of knots or beads at regular intervals along a line that appears to be straight.

Bird's eye stitch is just another variation of the old chain stitch. In this case it is used in any length, but was usually grouped around a center as when it was used to make the petal of a daisy in floral embroidery.

Blanket stitch is really just a widely spaced buttonhole stitch. This is the stitch that often was used to "finish" the edges of bridge cloths and baby blankets. After the hem was neatly put up, the entire edge or border was blanket-stitched in a matching or contrasting color of thread. A smaller version of this stitch was used on some appliqué.

Border stitch has a slight resemblance to the herringbone stitch, yet it is made quite differently. To make this stitch, make short stitches on the reverse side of the fabric and leave the longer thread to show on the right side. The stitch is worked perpendicularly rather than from left to right, which is one of the reasons it is different from the herringbone.

Brick couching stitch is one of the raised designs that has to be done on what grandma would have called a "stout" piece of fabric. The fabric had to be heavy and closely woven if much couching was to be done. To produce this stitch the cords were laid on the fabric in the desired design and stitched with fine cotton sewing thread. The couching was done by working silk or other types of embroidery thread across two cords in an alternating fashion that made the work look like laid bricks, hence the name.

Brick darning stitch was simply another stitch used to achieve a brick wall effect, and it usually was used as a background stitch. First lines were made by a running stitch of the same

Brick couching stitch.

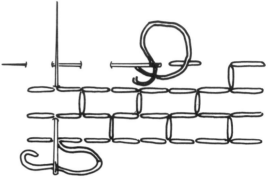

Brick darning stitch.

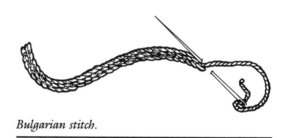

Bulgarian stitch.

length on both sides of the fabric on every other line. The lines between these would have alternate stitches and spaces. When the lines running lengthwise were completed, stitches of the same type were run crosswise to achieve the brickwork effect.

Bulgarian stitch was a fancy name for wide rows of embroidery made entirely of outline stitches. One row after another of outline stitch was worked to make part of the design like the stems of large flowers. It also was used to make the borders of petals in large designs. Known primarily as an outline stitch, it became a filling stitch when worked over large surfaces.

Bullion stitch, often called *gold bullion* in embroideries done in ancient times, is thought to have originated in Mycenae because remnants of it were found in the tombs there, but Turkey is credited with perfecting it. Not only were gold threads used in the old days, but solid bullion embroidery was simplified as well as made more elaborate with the use of gold spangles sewn tightly on the fabric. Some of the work was done with a tubular gold wire with a hole in the center through which the needle and thread could pass to fasten it to the fabric. Since most of the embroiderers could not afford the extra expense of the gold spangles and wires, they used an excellent Japanese or Turkish gold embroidery thread.

Plain silk embroidery thread worked well later with this stitch when it was laid on heavily in a similar stitch called satin stitch. Thread wrapped around a needle at least a dozen times and then left in a rope-like effect on top also was called a bullion stitch by Victorian embroiderers. Apparently the idea for using this later stitch was to make the work look lavish and extravagant without being wasteful, or to put it simply, "Keep it luxurious yet economical."

Buttonhole stitch was and still is a satin stitch with a flair. As a simple sewing stitch, it is used for the purpose for which it was named— to make handmade buttonholes. In embroidery it often was used on circles and especially on scallops. On some of the more elaborate pieces it was used to make the border. One piece of clothing that comes instantly to mind is the top of old corset covers, as the best of them always had scalloped tops finished in buttonhole stitch.

This is one of the few stitches that is easier to make and looks better when made by holding the work in one's hand rather than in embroidery hoops or a frame. As with satin stitch the thread is never knotted when making buttonhole stitches, instead it is used to make running stitches in the fabric—a sort of padding. The close work of the buttonhole stitch holds the ends of the thread. When the design is completed, that end of the thread is buried in the work. Embroiderers soon learned to estimate the correct amount of thread needed to make so many scallops, otherwise there would be many telltale places where new thread began. New thread ends can be buried under completed work once the embroiderer becomes experienced. This stitch was and is used to do cutwork.

Cable stitch is as easy and as fast as chain stitch, and differs from it only in the fact that the needle is inserted outside the preceding loop rather than in it. The needle is inserted just a fraction to the right of and below the preceding loop to form a chain of open loops.

Cable plait stitch was a very complicated stitch and as far as is known was used only on very elaborate designs, like in Mountmellick embroidery. The stitch is begun by bringing the needle and thread up on one side of the line, then the thread, usually silk, was held down with the left thumb and the needle was passed under the thread from right to left. It was drawn up until the thread under the thumb formed a small loop. The point of the needle was placed under the small loop, raising it to the line where the needle was inserted to bring out the point on the next line. The loop under the thumb was released and drawn around the top of the needle, which was then passed through the thread from left to right and then drawn through. Each stitch is made the same way so that it produces a thick so-called plait, hence the name. Since silk thread was generally used to make this stitch, problems arose with the thread twisting and knotting. One way to avoid that problem was to work slowly and carefully.

Cable plait and overcasting stitch was another one used only in the fancier designs. All that was necessary after the cable plait was completed was to do a stitch, here it is called an overcast, but in reality it is nothing more than a tent stitch in each plait.

Cat, brier, and coral stitches are all variations of the basic *feather stitch*. Also known in some areas as the seamstress feather stitch,

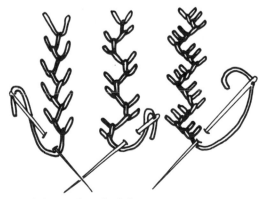

Cat, brier, and coral stitches.

these stitches often were used on crazy quilts and the velvet and silk patchwork quilts that were made and embroidered about a century ago. Since no design was necessary, the embroiderer simply drew a line to follow, if the surface was plain, or else followed the seams on the old quilts. Twisted thread was the preference for this stitch, especially on the quilts.

Chain stitch is thought to have been the first stitch ever used in embroidery. There are also many variations of this simple stitch, just as there are of most of the basic stitches. The chain is a series of loop stitches, with each growing out of the one before it. Each succeeding loop is taken through the lower end of the preceding one. The needle is put through the preceding loop just to the right of the thread already there, then through the fabric, and up again for the same distance as the preceding loop.

The simple *couching stitch* is thought to have originated during the fifteenth or sixteenth centuries by the very skilled Flemish embroiderers. There are several variations of this stitch, but the simple couching stitch consists of merely fastening one or more threads or cords to the ground fabric with small stitches taken at a right angle to the cord. Couching has been used to outline other embroidery, and with small gold threads it has been used to fill in backgrounds, especially in the beautiful embroideries that were made in China and Japan a century or so ago.

Cross-stitch was the first stitch taught to children in America, probably because it was and still is so easy. This is another stitch with many variations, some of them quite fancy and named accordingly. Cross-stitch is formed by sewing a series of diagonal stitches, then reversing the process to lay the next stitches of the same size in the opposite direction as the first. They should exactly form a cross.

A *darning stitch* is one of the most simple stitches in embroidery. It is a plain running stitch, yet it requires some practice because each row must have the same amount of tension. Simple though it may be, beginners have to practice to be able to space the stitches correctly. It consists of running many or only a few parallel lines of alternating stitches that are longer on the front of the fabric than on the back. The alternating rows should be worked so that the longer top lines center the shorter stitch or space between the two longer top stitches. This stitch was generally used for background work.

Diaper couching stitch is used on another stitch to form an original design and is more intricate than some stitches, therefore it was used more by advanced workers than by beginners. This stitch was never used except over the top of a design done in satin stitch. Once the satin stitch was completed using either silk cord or a twisted thread in long parallel lines, the couching began. Using the same type of thread that was used to do the satin stitch, the worker now twists it slightly, then crosses the design in an opposite angle from the way the satin stitch was made to form diamonds on the top. This is another form of stitchery that gives the worker great leeway in deciding how it will be used as the old-timers often made their designs as they went along.

Double chain stitch is one of the variations of the original chain stitch. In this case the embroiderer makes two rows of chain stitch about half an inch apart, then fills in the middle with a regular stitch that is passed through the inner edge of each of the two rows alternately. It gives the effect of a rope ladder slightly askew. This stitch often was used when embroidering in colors, with the chains made of one color and the center stitches of a contrasting color.

Double reverse chain stitch is not really as complicated as it sounds, but this is another stitch that requires much practice to master. Actually it is the reverse of what is usually done to make a chain stitch. One begins as with the simple chain stitch, but instead of putting the needle down the distance of the stitch below, it is inserted into the same loop or chain and brought out just to the right, almost exactly where the thread leaves the fabric. The needle is pulled through to make the stitch, then passed back of the simple stitch to form a double loop. The next stitch is made by putting the needle down to the left of the first stitch, then out again the length of the stitch.

Feather stitch is an old favorite that lends

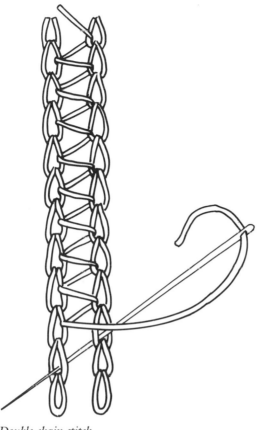

Double chain stitch.

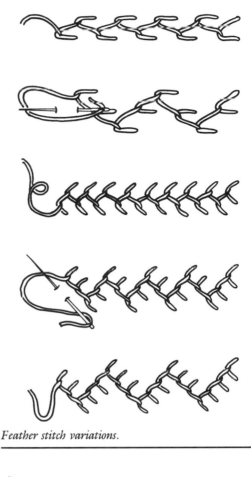

Feather stitch variations.

itself beautifully to many variations. To make a simple feather stitch, the needle is placed slightly to the right of where it came through the fabric the last time. It is then inserted to the left of that stitch, and the process begins all over again. The whole length of stitches is made by making a small stitch to the right and then to the left of an imaginary center. This is another stitch that was used frequently on the seams of the old velvet and silk patchwork quilts. Earlier a group called a type of work they did feather stitch, but it best could be described as a series of long and short stitches solidly laid to form a type of shadow work feather stitch. Most needleworkers in the last century or so have agreed that the first stitch is one almost universally recognized as plain feather stitch.

Fishnet stitch is a rather strange stitch that appears to be more like knotting thread than an actual stitch. It is very much like *honeycomb*

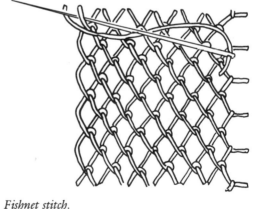

Fishnet stitch.

stitch and is made similar. To make the fishnet stitch only the first and last rows of thread are stitched to the fabric. The balance of the stitches, if they can be called stitches, are taken through the loops instead of the fabric. Each succeeding row pulls down on the loops in the preceding row so that when the bottom row is fastened, it stretches out to form a beautiful fishnet design.

French knot stitch, usually referred to simply as *French knots,* was another of the simple stitches taught young girls in the early days. As soon as she had mastered cross-stitch, she was ready to begin learning French knots. To make a French knot the thread is knotted before the needle is pushed through from the underside. This knotting is done in most embroidery stitches to prevent the thread from pulling through. With the needle and thread now on the top side of the fabric, the thread is wrapped around the point of the needle three times for an average-size French knot. Holding the thread firm but not too tight, the needle is inserted into the fabric two or three woven threads from the place where it first entered and is then pushed through to the wrong side. This forms a tiny circle of thread fastened on one side. When the thread was wrapped around the needle a dozen times or more and the "coil" laid flat, it was called a *bullion stitch* by some. For lighter fabrics a smaller knot is better so the thread is only wrapped around the needle once or twice.

Frilled basket stitch is another one that is used more by the advanced worker than by the beginner as it can get complicated. First, a cord is laid in a straight line. Then, using two silk threads, the embroiderer works back and forth, forming tiny loops on each side of the cord. When worked with the expensive gold thread, the so-called frills on either side give it an entirely different look.

Gobelin stitch was made famous by the Gobelin tapestries, and it was considered more a tapestry stitch than an embroidery stitch. But when done correctly, embroidered pieces are almost as pretty as the tapestries. Gobelin stitch is made by a series of satin stitched bars or squares worked adjacent to one another. The stitchery is not done quite as closely as the regular satin stitch.

From all indications, *Gordian knot stitch* was a new stitch introduced, at least in America, just before the turn of the century. Much of the fancy stitchery in those days was done with silk thread, and this was no exception. It was

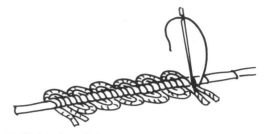

Frilled basket stitch.

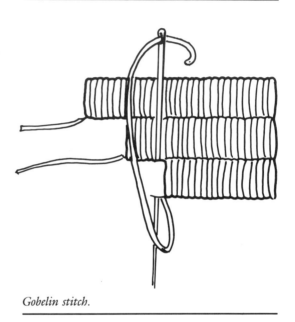

Gobelin stitch.

made by holding the thread under the left thumb while the needle was passed from right to left. With a little movement the thumb was used to push the thread under the point of the needle. All the thread was turned upward and the position of the needle reversed before it was inserted straight down through both the thread and the fabric. This formed a knot, and others were formed the same way about every fourth inch or so depending on the design.

Herringbone stitch is a type of cross-stitch that is made all at one time rather than returning over the same row. In this stitch the thread is crossed near the base rather than in the middle as is done in regular cross-stitch. The first stitch is a short one taken on the back from right to left. It is followed by an identical short stitch taken in the same direction at the bottom of the design and to the right of the first. This

Herringbone stitch.

Holbein stitch.

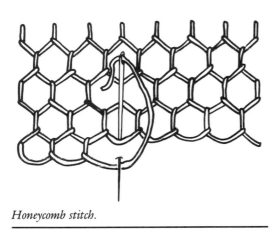

Honeycomb stitch.

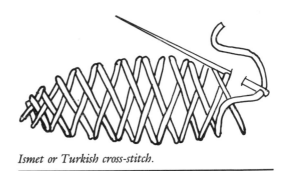

Ismet or Turkish cross-stitch.

creates a long stitch on the front of the fabric that is slanting from left to right. The next short underneath stitch should be in line horizontally with the first one so that when it is drawn through to make another long stitch it also will be on the top. In this stitch the threads cross near the top and at the base, not in the center.

Holbein stitch is actually the first stages of brick darning. Many of the stitches originated as simple ones, then a more skilled embroiderer would see the possibilities of adding a few extra stitches to create an entirely new as well as a fancier design. It is one of the simplest of stitches as it is only a running stitch going in both directions. This one also was used on tapestries. The first stitch is run in one direction with the second returning in the same stitch.

Honeycomb stitch is begun by making a row of wide buttonhole stitches about the width normally used around the sides of a baby blanket. Unlike the fishnet stitch, where the thread only enters the fabric on the first and last rows, each stitch of the honeycomb is taken through the fabric as well as through the row above it. It then comes out below where it forms a line of loops for the next row. This stitch is very adaptable, as it can be made smaller or larger as space and design demand.

Ismet cross-stitch, also called *Turkish cross-stitch,* is simply a way of describing cross-stitches worked closely and in ovals or scrolls. The effect is caused by the slight change in the way the Ismet stitch is worked. It is worked like the herringbone rather than the regular cross-stitch and is much wider. When it is worked closely, the threads can cross one another several times. When it is necessary to make the stitches extremely long, they can be fastened with a couching stitch at the intersections, somewhat like the short stitch used in diaper couching.

Janina cross-stitch is another of those stitches where the back or "wrong" side is as pretty as the "right" side. This stitch was very popular with the Turkish embroiderers, who excelled in the more intricate stitches. It was used particularly on leaves as it not only filled them in a sort of braid effect, but also created a different design than that produced by the outline or satin stitch normally used for leaves.

Kensington outline stitch is a sort of reverse back stitch with the stitches looking like a partly double line on the front and a series of small separate stitches on the back. To begin the stitch all the thread is brought to the front or top side, then the needle is pushed back into the fabric about an eighth of an inch above the point where it first entered. This process continues; each stitch is made exactly alike. On soft fabric it was sometimes difficult to get the correct tension on each stitch, but being able to make every stitch perfect was the secret of beautiful embroidery.

Long and short buttonhole stitch very well could have been a late creation as it seems it was used more on embroideries made during the past century. It was used predominately on borders and scallops as well as some leaves and flower petals. It is a variation of the regular buttonhole stitch, but is not worked as closely, and it is worked with a long stitch alternating with a shorter one.

Long and short cross-stitch can be any of a number of variations of regular cross-stitch. One variation was made by working long, slanting stitches, an inch or more if necessary or desirable, then making short horizontal stitchlike running stitches across the center. Another way to make them was to make the same slanting stitches with short stitches slanting in the opposite direction across the top and bottom of the long stitches. Yet another way was to use the short bottom stitches only. In the early days, when the embroiderer was finally left alone to create both her design and stitches, variations of the cross-stitch were many.

Long and short stitch is exactly what the name implies: a long stitch alternating with a short stitch. This stitch was used frequently in the early days to embroider a leaf similar to a grape or oak leaf, or petals with jagged or uneven edges. The stitches had to be close together but never overlapping. When using this stitch it was imperative that the outside line be kept absolutely true, and for that reason embroiderers were instructed to always begin and continue the work with the stitches one thread beyond the stamped line.

Pattern darning is a darning stitch used for backgrounds or borders. The lines are worked up and down or across, whichever is most effective. The stitch is the same as that used in darning (running parallel lines of alternating stitches with the longer ones on the top of the fabric).

Persian cross-stitch.

Persian cross-stitch was still another variation of the simple cross-stitch. These variations were given different names so written instructions could be universally understood. This began at a time when a large number of people began embroidering, of whom many were unable to create their own designs and stitches. A whole new industry sprang up to supply their needs, offering a variety of stamped and packaged linens and clothing along with the correct amount of thread needed to complete the article and instructions. Some needlework still is packaged that way, except we now call them kits. The name Persian cross-stitch may have been derived from the fact that this stitch was used on many of the old Persian embroideries. The Persians also are credited with creating this stitch. It was more a "filling" stitch than the regular cross-stitch, and was more difficult to execute. But it was well worth the extra effort to obtain the rich color designs.

Portuguese laid stitch was so called because it was found on so many embroidery pieces from that country. It can best be described as a sort of couching stitch. First, the groundwork is done by laying silk threads or cords in parallel lines about a quarter of an inch apart. Then the laid stitch is covered with a satin stitch that covers two of the threads for about six to eight inches. This makes embroidered spaces and blank spaces alternate so the fabric shows through.

Queen Anne darning stitch apparently originated in England and was named for the queen. It is a different stitch in that the thread was only worked into the fabric on the first round. The first step was to place long parallel lines of thread across the design. It can be laid closely for a closed effect or widely spaced for an airy effect. Both effects are beautiful, so it all depended on what the worker was trying to achieve. The first thread goes through the fabric. The next threads, usually silk, were woven over the first stitches at right angles. This thread was not passed through the fabric, only through the stitching in an over and under weaving process with the first lines. An embroidery hoop or frame was essential for this work as it had to be taut without being too tight.

Roman stitch could be called a double buttonhole stitch because it was made with two buttonhole stitches back to back. This stitch was used mainly for borders and was done by working one of the buttonhole stitches up and the next down. Both were done at the same time with one stitch made on the upper row and the next on the lower row, but they were joined in the middle with what might best be described as a row of braids. The width of this stitch can be increased or decreased without too much trouble. When the stitches are shortened it makes the braided center look wider.

Rope stitch is a heavy stitch that was used by many in preference to the couched cord. For one thing it was easier to make. To make it one begins with a loop, then each succeeding stitch is made by sending the needle down on the left and back to the loop rather than through the loop. The needle comes out on the right to form a heavy raised outline stitch. For best results the stitches should be short.

Satin stitch is another of the earliest stitches used in embroidery. It is easy to do, but a bit tedious. Practice is required to do it perfectly. It was used on much of the early church embroidery because the smooth satin look was exquisite. Satin stitch is simply filling any design with thread laid close, but never overlapping. In America the satin stitch was and still is used extensively for monogramming. Since it was the custom to monogram a good portion of the linens in the early dower or marriage chest, the satin stitch became famous.

Seed stitch is a very confusing name for a simple stitch that is actually the reverse of the darning stitch. There is some question as to why it was named and included in the lists of stitches in the first place. All experienced embroiderers were able to adjust or vary stitches to fit their needs, so it is possible this was another of the stitches that was given a name so

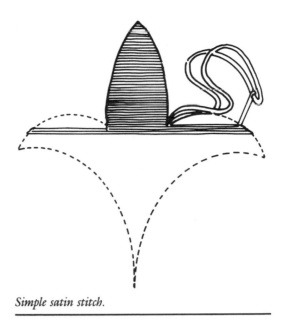

Simple satin stitch.

it could be used in written instructions. This is a popular stitch outlining the letters for monogramming since only the short stitch is seen on the front. The long part of the stitch is on the back.

Snail trail stitch was one of the few stitches where knots and loops were formed along a straight line. This stitch is made by carrying a stitch across the line and through the loop in the thread. The loops can be made at any distance, but are more effective when placed about every half inch. The finished work looks very much like a small snail trail.

Split stitch is in effect an outline stitch with the top thread split with the needle. When the needle is put in the fabric to make the next outline stitch, it is placed as nearly as possible in the center of the previous stitch, thereby "splitting" the thread. This is another stitch that required the use of hoops or a frame as the thread never was pulled too tight.

Tapestry stitch was the name given to satin stitch when it was used to fill in the background of large pieces. About the only difference in the stitches is that tapestry work was done in straight rows all running in the same direction. It was much easier to shade the work (use various shades of thread in one design when using this stitch). It also made a very luxurious garment, and it was very important in those early days that every effort be made to insure that church vestments looked rich and elegant. When the backgrounds of those vestments were filled with tapestry stitches done in rich gold and silver threads, they were beautiful indeed.

Tent stitch was so simple and so nearly useless that it is surprising it was even given a name. Although it was seldom used, apparently it was included in case it ever *was* used. The stitch is nothing more than a series of diagonal stitches, and was used to teach children accuracy in their first embroidery lessons.

Thorn stitch, like so many of the fancy stitches, was actually a combination of two or more well-known stitches. In this case the finished stitch looks like a feather stitch with a chain stitch between each "feather." As the thread is brought down for each alternating stitch, the worker makes a chain stitch rather than the regular feather stitch.

Twisted couching stitch is exactly what the name implies. The cords are twisted as they are couched in place. This is only a slight variation of the regular couching stitch, but can produce beautiful effects when used with it.

Twisted outline stitch is one of the more complicated stitches, and probably for that reason was not used very frequently. Twisted thread would not produce the desired results, therefore the worker twisted the thread as she made her stitches. Although a hoop could be used when doing this stitch, the work was never as satisfactory as when a frame was used. Using a double thread, the needleworker brought the full length of the thread to the top, where the needle was turned between her fingers until the thread was well twisted. The twisted thread then was held over the forefinger of the left hand while the right hand was used to put the needle back through the fabric, about a quarter of an inch above the line. It then was brought back through the fabric beside that stitch, then down through the fabric again. This stitch was used mostly for stems.

Wheat ear stitch is a combination of several stitches and looks like a fancy feather stitch. The single chain stitch is made, then a slanting stitch similar to the tent stitch is made on either side, then another chain and more tent stitches follow. This process continued until the design was completed.

Some of these stitches probably haven't been used for years, and when they are used now they may be known by a different name. All the information for these stitches was gleaned from old turn-of-the-century needlework books and magazines. Even they didn't agree on all the names.

CHAPTER 3

Preparation and Design

The art of embroidery has been practiced continuously since its creation. Sometimes there were only the dedicated few, who continued to ply their needles regardless of the trends, and at other times it seemed that everyone who could hold a needle was making some type of embroidery. From the eleventh to the fourteenth centuries, when the work was done exclusively in the monasteries and convents, each embroiderer was an expert or a student practicing to be an expert. This was a time when the girls of the parish as well as all homeless children were sent to the convent to learn embroidery. The items they made were for use either in the church or by the clergy. As the children returned to life outside, they were adept with their needles and began making items for sale to anyone who could afford them.

Prices were rather high for that time, therefore only members of the royal families and the wealthier people of the parish could afford to purchase these creations. As with anything new, the idea spread, and soon everybody who could afford it wanted some embroidery on their clothing. There always had been a small amount of embroidery used on garments since early Biblical times, but now there were skilled workers who could make garments rich with embroidery, provided the owner could afford them.

In no time at all it became a status symbol for all ladies to learn and practice some kind of needlework. The ladies of the royal families were as eager and as willing to learn as the masses. It became so fashionable to engage in some type of needlework that many old paintings show ladies posing while doing embroidery or perhaps tatting. It became the socially acceptable thing to do.

During the seventeenth and eighteenth centuries families migrated to the colonies in the New World. There some embroidery

Ladies often carried folding chairs like this when they went to help a neighbor "get out" a quilt or just do needlework.

would be done, but for nearly a century the most important thing on the minds of the newcomers was survival and getting settled—in that order. As more families arrived and more land was cleared and settled, the people settled into regular routines. Some engaged in businesses in the towns that were being settled. The wives of these men had more leisure time to pursue their needlework.

As permanent homes began to spring up all over the country, thoughts turned to making them more attractive. Since most of them could at least do the simple stitches, they began to use embroidery on their homespun fabric in an effort, no doubt, to add a bit of color to an otherwise drab house. The wives of businessmen and wealthy planters continued to order their embroidery materials from England.

At the same time, these women were teaching their children the joy of embroidery, as witnessed by the large amount of old samplers that are available. Some of those talented children grew up to devise and combine various stitches to make some of the most beautiful household linens known.

Americans are credited with adapting embroidery to use on all household linens. Embroidered linens were made and used in most of the countries of Europe, but never to the extent they were in America. Whereas Europeans had embroidered bed hangings, tablecloths, covers for both chairs and footstools, and cupboard cloths, Americans embroidered all these things as well as their dish towels. Few records have been found that describe the embroidery being used extravagantly on clothing during the first century or so in America, but once needleworking caught on, it mushroomed. Ladies embroidered every garment they wore, from their dresses to their underwear. Among the old clothing found today there will always be stacks of blouses, dresses, old pantaloons or drawers, chemises, and petticoats covered with tucks, tatting, embroidery, and various laces.

The Civil War had a drastic effect on needlework. Everything was geared to the war effort, which left very little time for needlework and even less material with which to do it. In the South, where most of the cotton was grown, many men had gone to war and the Southern economy and land were increasingly devastated as the war progressed. Without the cotton there was less fiber with which to make fabric. Apparently, the shortage of American cotton had a drastic effect on the world supply of cotton fabrics. It is not known whether it was a lack of materials, lack of interest in embroidery in general, or simply a lack of time that caused reporters at the 1861 London Exposition to state that the paucity of good needlework and the inferior quality shown "demonstrates the depths of degradation to which the domestic art of embroidery has fallen."

Like all arts and crafts, needlework—and especially embroidery—has had its highs and lows in popularity. The Civil War era just happened to be one of the lows that could be attributed to domestic problems. But a comeback was in the works. Around 1870–1875 all types of needlework began to experience a revival beyond anything ever seen before. This revival lasted for well over half a century.

During this revival volumes were published telling what kinds of embroidery to make and giving explicit directions on how to make them. Magazines were developed for the express purpose of catering to the needleworker, and told her not only how to make the various items of clothing and household linens, but also exactly where to find the necessary supplies and equipment. What once had been a work of dedication, with embroiderers sitting day after day plying their needles, was now touted as "pick-up work." As the housewife took a few minutes to rock the baby to sleep, she could rock the cradle with her foot while doing a few stitches on a new piece of embroidery. At night, as she rested before the fire, she could pick up her needlework and do a few more stitches. The piece was not completed as quickly as it would have been had she worked steadily, nor did the work display the excellent quality it once had, but she was embroidering nonetheless.

Some of the more fortunate women did have enough spare time to spend hours on their needlework, and they created some exquisite items. Some of the more talented ones and those with enough time made pieces for their own homes and made gifts for friends and relatives. Some even made pieces to sell to less-talented friends. This way they were able to make enough money to buy more materials and maybe earn some pin money as well.

Many of the early writers who wrote lengthy articles for the various needlework magazines were themselves experienced needleworkers, and they were constantly striving to upgrade both the methods and the types of work done. They encouraged all embroiderers to strive for the correct colors and shading to give each colored flower design a more realistic look. Much thought and planning went into every piece of needlework. Of course there were exceptions, but generally most of the work was good. Then there were those pieces made for special occasions or with a special use, like the "dining room set" that was the equivalent of our present-day place mats, except the dining room sets had many more pieces.

It was the accepted custom among genteel people at that time to use a large embroidered linen tablecloth on the table for dinner or the evening meal when the family was together. Doilies, in assorted sizes for each dish, were acceptable for breakfast and the tea table. Soon it became fashionable to use doilies for lunch. The doilies that made up the dining room set usually consisted of no less than three (and usually more) different-sized doilies for each place. One was for the service or luncheon plate, another for the bread and butter plate, while the third was for the tumbler. The sets never were made in less than service for four, and were usually in sets of at least a dozen. Remember, this was a time when families were large and there was much entertaining.

If time and money were no problem and the housewife was skilled with the needle, she often would make dozens of different sets of doilies. The plainer ones were used by the family for "everyday use" while the more elaborate ones were saved for guests or holidays.

In many of the sets that made up the "linens for the dining room," the embroiderer went to great lengths to use colors for the embroidery that would match perfectly the colors in her china. Assorted shades of blue thread was used on white linens for those with sets of china in either flow blue or delft blue. Many preferred their linens done in white-on-white (white embroidery on white fabric), as they felt this could be used with any and all china. Then there were those who liked variety and embroidered their linens or at least some of their linens in soft shades of pink, yellow, blue and green—the predominate colors in Haviland china. Mixing and matching too many colors in the dining room was not in the best taste, some said, so they kept most of the colors soft and muted.

Every now and then they would go wild with colors, and one of the prettiest examples of that work was a three-piece set of doilies embroidered with a fruit design. Unlike most of the work using fruit designs, this one was not done in satin stitch, but was done solidly in French knots. The work was enhanced with the use of several shades of thread in each piece of fruit to make it more realistic in appearance. For instance, the peaches were done partly in an orange-red with yellow shading to nearly cream on one side. Of course, the grapes were all in rich, royal purple just as they would be when ripe and still on the vine. The outline of the grapes was in the same shade of purple. The pears were works of art with the embroidery having been done in two shades of light brown or beige. The lighter shade, which was only a shade darker than ecru, was used near the top and the bottom was done in the slightly darker color. A cream-colored thread was used to make the French knots that filled the blossoms, and they were outlined in the same color. All the French knots were average in size (about three threads around the needle), and were placed closely in the design but not crowded. The background fabric was barely visible, yet it made the design stand out beautifully. The stems and leaves were done in a satin stitch using green for the leaves and brown for the stems.

Since American embroiderers have been credited with the general adaptation of embroidery to household linens, some of the early authorities seemed to think that the standard of work was lower in this country. There is little doubt it was not as elaborate as that made in the convents, but American needlework was made for everyday use in the home (in most cases), while the early embroidery made in the convents was for church use only. There the workers had nothing to do except needlework; in America the housewife had a family to raise, chores to do, and in some instances had to help her husband with the business or with the farm work while still trying to create pretty linens for her home. Naturally there would be a difference in quality if the work was judged on merit alone.

Then there were those who felt that the embroidered household linens helped to bring "an uplifting influence of such art into everyday life." Perhaps this was true as early life in America was hard on those early settlers, especially those who migrated south and west, and their household furnishings drab unless brightened with colorful needlework.

Not only were Americans credited with adapting embroidery to household linens, but out of necessity they devised ways and means for making it easier. In those days there were no stamped designs as we know them today. At that time the worker could either gauge her design by counting threads or she could draw a design of sorts, then fill it in to the best of her ability. Later these ingenious ladies discovered a way to reproduce or transfer the design from a finished piece of embroidery to a new piece of fabric. The finished piece was laid on a smooth surface and covered with the fabric on which the worker would transfer the design. First, she would rub the smooth top of a snuff box (nearly all ladies dipped snuff in those days) over her long hair, then over the two pieces while being careful to hold both firmly in place. Either the oil or dirt from her hair caused the design to show up on the new fabric in good detail as she continued to rub the snuff box over her hair and then over the fabric.

\ Counted stitch embroidery currently is experiencing a big revival and has a long history of popularity. In the old days about the only stitches that could be used easily when counting threads were couching and cross-stitch. The latter was made across three to

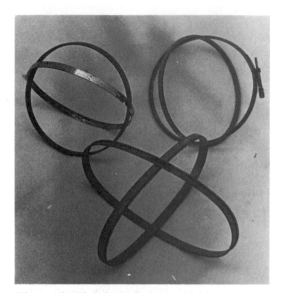

Three embroidery hoops, both round and oblong.

Wooden embroidery hoop with adjustable button.

seven threads, depending on the size of the stitches wanted and the weave of the fabric.

For decades there had been embroidery frames in Europe, but an American manufacturer made one that resembled a small quilting frame and sold it at a price everyone could afford: one dollar. Like the quilting frame, it was fastened with screws and clamps on the corners and could be taken apart for storage. Many a husband simply copied the frame and made his wife an assortment of frames in various sizes.

The fabric with the design drawn on (and later the stamped pieces) was sewn with wide and long overcast-type stitches onto the

Late hand-painted thimble in sweet-grass woven thimble holder.

frame—very much like "putting up" a quilt. The piece was securely fastened to the frame in a taut position with all the edges straight.

The advantage of the embroidery frame over conventional hoops was that the work stayed in one position instead of being moved many times as the work progressed. The fabric stayed cleaner in the frame because it was handled less, and the stitches were more even because the embroiderer could judge how tight to pull the threads as she viewed the overall work. Although the frames were described as having more advantages, most needleworkers continued to use hoops. Embroidery hoops can be found in antiques shops today made of wood, metal, or a combination of the two materials. Old ones are plentiful for the collector who just wants a few to complete the "needlework scene." Prices for hoops are still quite low.

Actually, many exquisite pieces of embroidery were made with only a needle and thread. Frames and hoops (and thimbles that were made in a variety of styles and materials)

were nice, and most people used them, but none of them were absolutely essential to the skilled needleworker.

One older embroiderer who has never used a thimble yet has created some elegant pieces of needlework explained the reason she doesn't use a thimble. When she was being taught to embroider, she says, there weren't enough thimbles to go around—there were more girls than thimbles in the family. Since she was the oldest, she let the younger girls have the thimbles in the hopes they would learn to do needlework correctly. In later years, when she was able to afford one, she found that using a thimble was uncomfortable.

Scissors of some type are necessary in needlework if for nothing else than cutting threads. Of course one could and still does use regular scissors, but during the heyday of needlework, manufacturers flooded the market with scissors of all types, each made for a specific job. Embroidery scissors, always small, were made in a variety of styles and materials, including ones featuring sterling silver handles. Buttonhole scissors originally designed to cut the fabric inside the worked buttonhole were later used for cutwork.

Sewing tables were quite an asset for the needleworker. Not only could she attach her hoops to the side, but she also could store her

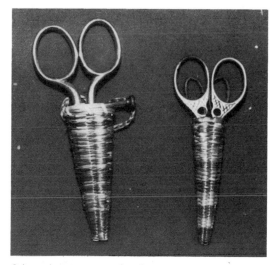

Scissors in sweet-grass sheaths.

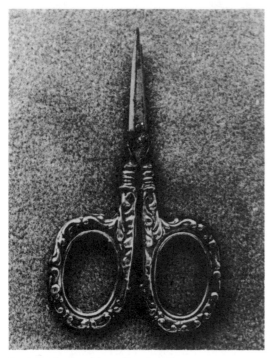

Sewing scissors with sterling handles.

Around 1900 and for a few decades afterward, the Passamaquoddy Indians made these ash splint sewing stands to sell to the tourists in Maine.

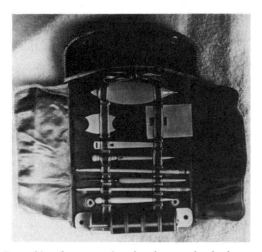

Everything from a tatting shuttle to crochet hooks were in this case of celluloid sewing tools.

fabrics and threads in the deep drawer and keep needles, pins, thimbles, and scissors in the shallow drawer.

Sewing boxes or workboxes, long popular in England, began to find their way into American homes, but here the sewing basket was more popular in most areas, especially in later years. Sewing cases filled with scissors, needlecases, thimbles, and assorted tools were offered in sterling silver, silver plate, and later in celluloid.

Special lights were used by some of the old lacemakers, but as far as is known no special light or lights were made specifically for embroiderers. Light was very necessary for their work and we can rest assured that they devised some method of lighting for their work, whether it was from a candle or a lamp.

All of these tools, along with the needlework they made, can be found in shops, antiques shows, and malls today at very reasonable prices.

Ash splint sewing basket made by the Passamaquoddy Indians.

For a decade before and after the turn of the century, wicker sewing stands were extremely popular.

CHAPTER 4
Needles, Threads, and Pins

Needles are one of mankind's oldest tools, yet information on their origin and early history is limited. It is believed that sewing was first done by boring holes in fabric or animal skins with awls made of bone, flint, or thorns, and then sinew from animals laced through the holes. Indications are that through the years every conceivable material known—including wood, bone, shell, iron, bronze, and gold and silver—was hammered into slender instruments that would carry the thread back and forth through the fabric. The gold and silver needles must have been complete disasters, especially the gold ones. Without some other material or alloy mixed with them, they are quite soft and would be unuseable. Later, one of the most desirable types of needles had gold eyes. Apparently only the eye of the completed needle was washed or plated with gold.

The Bantu-speaking people of Africa are credited with making a needle of iron or steel that had a slightly depressed area directly under the pinlike head where the thread could be tied. Thread was tied around the needle rather than passed through an eye. In fact, this idea was probably the forerunner of the pin. It is small wonder that much of the early wearing apparel seemed to be draped rather than shaped by sewing.

It is believed that the Chinese were the first to discover ways to make needles of steel, and the method is believed to have been carried to Europe by the Moors. By this time needles had become a very necessary tool, and since they had not yet been perfected, each inventor was positive he had devised the perfect sewing needle. From around 1375 to after 1400, Nuremberg was the accepted capital of needlemaking. During the next century it was England's turn to be the leader of this industry, but not until after 1650 did needle making become an important industry there. It is known that around that time and for a while thereafter the needlemakers established their shops near those of the tailors and dressmakers. The area of London where they settled became known as Threeneedle Street, but has long since become known as Threadneedle Street.

Needles with eyes were known during the mid-1700s. Miss Mary Linwood, who spent sixty of her ninety years embroidering copies of great old paintings, said in an interview in 1785 that she "had executed (the pictures) with fine crewels dyed under her supervision and worked on thick tammy woven especially for her sixty-four pictures that were exact replicas of paintings done by Gainsborough and others." They had been drawn entirely by her and embroidered without assistance of any kind, even on the backgrounds. The only assistance she ever received, she said, "was in the threading of her needles." Some of those embroidered pictures, which attracted the attention of the royal family, were sold in 1845 by Christie and Manson, London auctioneers, for around £4,000.

In 1826 a stamping machine was invented that would produce a needle with a drilled eye, but it would be nearly another half century before a machine would be introduced that would do most of the work mechanically. It would be another decade or so (circa 1885) before the needles would be completely finished by machine.

Before this latest invention needles were made individually, yet it sounds like mass production when reports are found that one man could flatten as many as 2500 needles a day.

The large-scale needle industry finally seemed to settle in Redditch, England, but before that happened each country would claim one or more needle factories. As the quality of the needles made at Redditch became known, embroiderers as well as other needle workers began to prefer them. Slowly, the other factories began to disappear while Redditch grew larger.

Since the needle was the tool that made the stitches, embroiderers were careful to choose the right size for the thread and fabric to be used. It was soon found that the gold-eyed needles would not cut the thread. Hence, they became favored, especially when using silk thread. At that time the most popular embroidery threads were Filo silk, Persian floss, etching silk, Roman floss, and rope silk. A chenille needle was described as the choice for use with rope silk.

Various suggestions have been offered for how to select the correct size of needle for use on various types of work, but one old rule, "If the silk (thread) starts roughing up, you will know the needle you are using is too small," seems to provide the best advice.

Small though it may be, the needle has been recognized as one of the most important tools, not just for fancy needlework, but for tailoring and dressmaking as well. Reference to it is made several times in the Bible. One verse, "It is easier for a camel to go through the eye of a needle, than for a rich man to enter into the kingdom of God," is repeated in three different places—proof enough that by Biblical times the needle had some type of eye.

Needles were mentioned in the writings of Holmes and Shakespeare, among others. They also were mentioned in a few Mother Goose nursery rhymes. Perhaps the best known is "Needles and pins, needles and pins, When a man marries his troubles begin."

As soon as machines that could complete a needle in a single operation were developed,

Inside of old needle case just as it came from the Redditch factory.

Collecting advertising cards was popular before the turn of the century, and none were more plentiful than those issued by the thread companies.

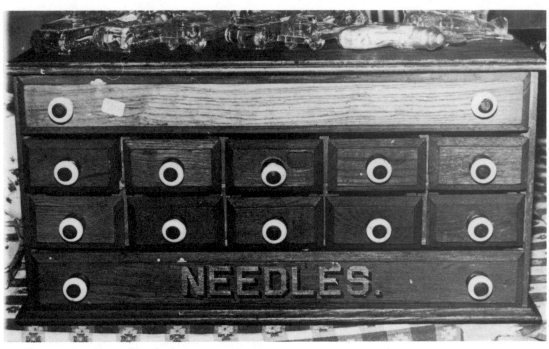

Needle cases also were used in the stores.

factories began to be established. Manufacturers then began giving thought to packaging the needles. For years packages and boxes of English needles carried a portrait of Queen Victoria. These are very collectible now because they are very scarce. The later packages that featured colorful lithographed pictures and were issued around the turn of the century are now being collected. So far, the demand is not that strong, but they do add to a display of old clothing and linens.

Originally, needles were quite expensive, therefore embroiderers were very concerned about containers and storage. This prompted the development of the needle case. Today needle cases can be found made of every conceivable material, from sterling silver to celluloid. Of the old cases, ones made of ivory and imitation ivory seem most plentiful. Cases were made of mother-of-pearl; more-expensive ones were made of enamels after the cloisonné style. Among the very scarce and expensive needle cases are early ones inlaid with silver and gold. Some even had precious stones set in the designs.

Needle books also became quite popular.

Birch bark needle case laced with ribbon. Made for Maine tourist trade circa 1900.

Some of the embroiderers made their own needle books using fancy embroidered covers while others preferred to crochet or tat a cover. Some needle books were done in perforated card work. In later years merchants often gave

Contemporary sweet-grass needle case made by the Mohawk Indians.

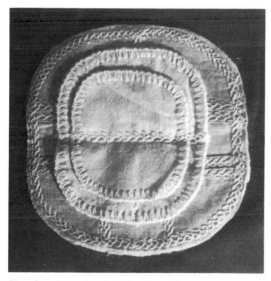

Handmade and embroidered needle case, open.

Fancy cabinets were used to display silk thread in many stores.

pretty packages of needles to special customers as an advertising gimmick.

The first thread used for stitching was the sinew of animals. However, as soon as women learned to spin thread from wool, flax, or cotton, these types of thread were mixed with a little gold, silver, or silk thread for effect. Silk thread was so beautiful and luxurious as well as strong, elastic, and durable that it soon became the favorite of embroiderers.

Even the history of silk is romantic. According to legend it all began with Hoang-ti, the third emperor of China, who lived and ruled around 1700 B.C. Being an inquisitive person, he began to wonder if anything could be made from the many cocoons spun by the silkworms. With the help of his fourteen-year-old empress, Sing Li Chi, they began to cultivate the silkworms. After a long period of trial and error, she finally was able to discover the correct way to unwind the cocoons. Shortly thereafter a method for weaving the threads into fabric was discovered. In appreciation for her work and dedication, the people of China always referred to Sing Li Chi as the "Goddess of the Silkworm."

The Chinese soon discovered that the tiny silk threads made fabric that was soft, sheer, and gorgeous. They felt it was fit only for royalty—and actually they were about the only ones who could afford it. For many years a death penalty was imposed on anyone who

Skein winder.

tried to take either the silkworm or the eggs out of China. One could be put to death, according to the legend, for simply revealing the secret of silkworm culture or how the threads were unwound.

But eventually the Chinese did begin to sell some silk outside of China. Persia was one of the first countries to buy Chinese silk. It was later sold in Rome, and according to stories and legends, the Roman emperors felt the fabric was too luxurious for any except those of noble birth. Hence, it again was decreed that the average person could not wear silk. They probably couldn't have afforded it anyway.

Silk fabric was so expensive at that time that it was sold for gold only, and then on a weight-for-weight basis (one ounce of silk sold for one ounce of gold).

But the silkworm and its culture finally left China and arrived in Japan. Early in the sixth century, as the story goes, two monks told Byzantine emperor Justinian about the silk culture they had seen in China. He bribed the monks to return and smuggle out some eggs along with information on all phases of silk making. Around 555 A.D. the monks returned with the hollow sections of their bamboo canes filled with silkworm eggs.

The silk industry is reported to have reached Spain in approximately the eighth century, but it would be another eight centuries before it spread to Italy. It would be yet another century before the information would reach enough interested people in France.

From France it was a simple matter to get it to England. In fact, it was taken there by Flemish weavers. King James I was so convinced that silk would prove to be one of the successful new industries in the colonies that he sent a bountiful supply of silkworms and mulberry trees to Virginia. It didn't work in Virginia, but that didn't stop the settlers in Georgia, where it was found they would grow better. By the time they found out how to grow the silkworms easily and successfully, the cost of labor for unwinding the cocoons had risen so sharply that the American market was unable to compete with the cheaper Chinese market.

Silk thread was used exclusively for embroidering baby clothes, ladies' underwear, and some of the household linens. The choice of thread depended to a great extent on the type of fabric being used and the purpose for which the item was being made. For fancy, showy things silk was the first choice, but for

Another type of thread cabinet.

everyday linens cheaper cotton thread was satisfactory.

Up until about the eighteenth century, when thread-making machines were invented, women who could spin a small thread, one that was even in texture and fine enough to use for hand sewing as well as embroidery, were extremely popular and could sell all the extra thread they could spin.

Cotton thread was cheaper and easier to work with, but a problem arose with the packaging. At that time thread was kept on thread winders—little gadgets made of ivory, tortoiseshell, wood, silver, and other materials

Old thread cabinets from country stores are sought after today. When legs are added, they become tables with many drawers.

31

with notches around them on which to wind the thread. The problem with winding cotton thread on a thread winder was the fact that it would become loose and tangle with other winders. In an effort to eliminate the problem, the so-called cotton barrel was made. The barrel consisted of a hollow container (usually made of wood) that could be either barrel- or egg-shaped with a spindle in the center. At one time it was the custom to return the spindle to the factory for refilling when all the thread had been used. The cotton barrel was more popular in England than it was in America.

Perhaps one of the reasons for the unpopularity of linen thread at that time was the fact that it was almost impossible to find it spun smooth and fine enough for general use. In the convents, when a girl appeared to have both talent and patience, she often was taught to spin the flax into fine thread. Even in later years, convent-spun linen thread never was offered for sale to the public.

Thread can then be "credited" with the invention of the thread winders, cotton barrels, and in later years the spool caddies. When thread was spun in the homes and convents, the spinning wheel, flax wheel, cards, yarn winders, and swifts were essential tools.

Waxing thread for both embroidery and beading is almost as old as stitchery. This in

Embroidered pincushion of English origin.

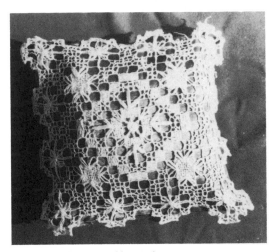

Lace pincushion over blue satin.

Homemade pincushion with drawer for sewing tools. It could be fastened on the arm of a chair.

Crocheted pincushion.

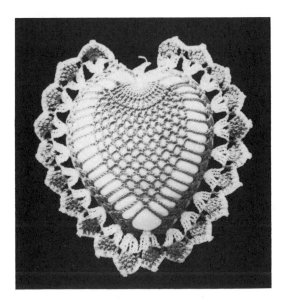

Late pincushion and spool rack patterned after those made earlier by the Shakers.

Velvet-topped sweet-grass pincushions are still being made by the Mohawk Indians.

Advertising card showing embroidery done by the Davis sewing machine.

turn created a need for a container for the wax so it could be kept in the sewing stand or basket. The wax could be used in a waxer or it could be molded into small decorated cakes of wax. If the family had several hives of bees, the wife often sold her extra wax to needleworkers in the city.

Later a refined wax was sold by most stores carrying needlework supplies. It is not unusual today to find an old waxer with portions of almost dried wax still in it. During the Victorian era, when needlework enjoyed its greatest popularity, thread waxers were made of ivory, imitation ivory, silver plate, sterling silver, wood, and tortoiseshell.

Pins are seldom thought of as essential to embroidery, and it is easy to work without them, but they are quite handy in pinning pieces in place or putting hems in tablecloths or drawn work. They are absolutely vital in lace making of the pillow variety because it would be impossible to pin the pattern without them.

The phrase "pin money" developed because at one time pins were so expensive

Hemming bird, often called a sewing bird.

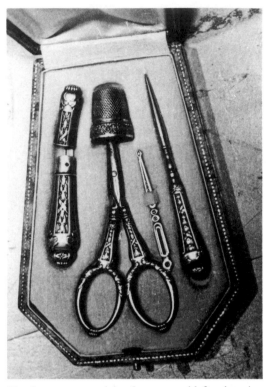

Big department and jewelry stores sold fitted sewing cases. They usually included stilettoes, bodkins, thimbles, scissors, and needle cases, often in sterling.

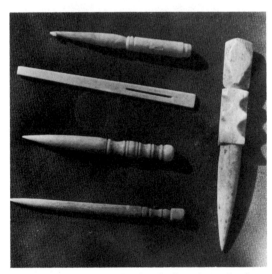

From top to bottom: Crochet hook (minus the fancy handle), bodkin, and three stilettoes.

Sterling silver tape measure.

money that had to be set aside for their purchase. Addison defined the term "pin money" as "a sum allowed or settled on a wife for her private expenses." With the high costs of pins at that time, a good deal of her allowance could have gone to buy pins.

Pins have changed little in all the centuries they have been made, and the reason is simple: Because of their small size, there is little room for designing new shapes and styles. The most noticeable difference has been in the manufacturing processes.

The first pins had heads made of minute coils of fine wire; later they had a round or ball head. Small thought they might be, the manufacture of pins became such a big operation in England that labor leaders used them 1825 to

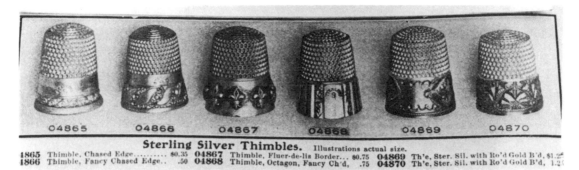

Sterling Silver Thimbles. Illustrations actual size.

| 04865 | 04866 | 04867 | 04868 | 04869 | 04870 |

4865 Thimble, Chased Edge.......... $0.35 **04867** Thimble, Fluer-de-lis Border... $0.75 **04869** Th'e, Ster. Sil. with Ro'd Gold B'd, $1.25
4866 Thimble, Fancy Chased Edge.. .50 **04868** Thimble, Octagon, Fancy Ch'd, .75 **04870** Th'e, Ster. Sil. with Ro'd Gold B'd, 1.25

Sterling silver thimbles could be bought for prices ranging from 35¢ to $1.25 in 1900.

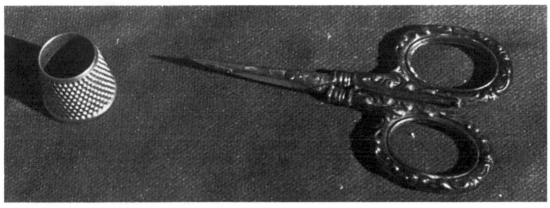

Sterling-handled embroidery scissors with tailor's thimble.

Sewing stand from the 1930s.

show the advantages of divisions of labor. Making the head alone required several operations. In fact, to make a pin at that time required eighteen separate operations.

Seventeen years later the Wright pinmaking machine would be developed and a pin would be made in a single operation. This simple operation won worldwide recognition because it reduced the cost of pins considerably. Progress continued until the time required to make a pin was only about one-fifth of a second.

Around 1875 the largest pin factory in the world was the Newhall Works, Birmingham, England, where production averaged ten million pins a day.

Today there is little left of those old pins except for memories and lots of old pincushions. Some of those old pincushions are not only very collectable, but they are

Silver-plated tape measure with notation, "Pull my head, but not my leg."

Rotary sewing stand with place for scissors, thimble, and spools of thread. There is a velour pincushion around the thimble holder.

exquisite as well. This includes the embroidered, crocheted, knitted, tatted, and beaded ones, which can be found in every shape, color, size, and material with workmanship ranging from poor to excellent.

After the invention of the sewing machine, at least one make, the Davis, was widely advertised as one on which "machine embroidery" could be made. Whether it was too expensive, too difficult to use, or the ladies just preferred handmade embroidery is unknown. No old pieces have been found that would suggest they were made on a sewing machine. The small amounts of machine-made embroidery available among the older pieces appear to have been factory-made.

Although we recognize that embroidery could be made with only a needle and thread, other items were necessary to make the work easier and prettier. These tools or accessories were used with all types of needlework, not just embroidery. The list includes bodkins, cotton barrels, embroidery frames and hoops, emery cases, needle books and cases, packaged needles, pins and pincushions, sewing cases, tables, sewing rockers, sewing birds, scissors, scissor sheaths, stilletos, tape measures, thread caddies, winders, thimbles, waxers, work stands, workboxes, and work baskets.

CHAPTER 5
Embroidered Fabrics

The majority of the old clothing and household linens found today were made during the better part of the Victorian era and on into the Roaring Twenties. This was the fifty-year period when embroidery experienced an unprecedented revival of interest. Around the turn of the century, the ladies were embroidering everything from teddies (underwear) to tablecloths. They were using any type of material—nothing seems to be too thick or too thin. Velvet baby caps were lined with the sheerest georgette and embroidered with rosebuds. Neither denim nor chamois were considered too thick or difficult to work with, as both were not only recommended but also were used extensively for a variety of items.

Most fabrics were made of silk, linen, cotton, or wool in those days, but nobody would have been caught dead asking for mere cotton or silk. They asked for it by a specific name, preferably a fancy one such as batiste or damask. Many of these materials are no longer made, but is is hoped that with these descriptions collectors of old needlework will be able to reasonably determine the type of material used in the various pieces they find. Then there were fabrics like muslin, nainsook, and batiste that were made in so many grades and were so similar that it is next to impossible to say with certainty which is which. The following fabrics are known to have been made into clothing or household linens or both and to have been profusely embroidered.

Batiste is the French name for *cambric,* a type of fine linen. It was named for a linen weaver named Baptista who is credited with its development circa 1275. Later batiste was made predominately of cotton except for the fine linen grades that could be obtained by special order. The expense of these fine grades removed it from regular stock. Cotton batiste might have been a thin fabric, but it was used to make everything from baby dresses to bedspreads.

Burlap is a loosely woven fabric commonly used for making feed bags, but it was used by some embroiderers who used the loose weaving to their advantage in counting threads for cross-stitch. This was used mainly to make curtains with embroidered borders and to make the desk sets that were glued on cardboard.

Cambric was the name for material equivalent to batiste, but it was made in England rather than France. Apparently the English fabric took its name from the town of Cambrai, where it was first made in France. In time it was made in Ireland, Scotland, and probably all countries that grew cotton as the cotton cambric became much more popular than the linen. As early as 1846, Wamsutta Mills of New Bedford, Massachusetts, produced cotton fabrics. Of the nineteen thousand bales of cotton used by the factory that year, about half went into the production of cambric.

Challis was a lightweight fabric of French origin that was first made of silk and wool and later of cotton and rayon.

Chamois was the original name given to the skin of an Alpine goat that had been cured using lime and repeated washings instead of salt, alum, and tan. Later the skins of deer, sheep, and ordinary goats would be cured with oil and sold as chamois. Chamois was used to make cigar cases that could be embroidered. Bill books, made to hold paper money, also were embroidered. When found today these bill books will be considerably larger than today's paper money because the old bills were almost twice the size of our present paper currency.

Shirt cases and traveling cases were embroidered as well. The latter was a homemade, hand-embroidered version of the later fitted traveling cases. All the items made for men were embroidered, but not as lavishly as pieces made for the ladies. It was suggested that makers of the traveling cases use oiled silk to make the pockets for the toothbrush and lotions. Chamois also was used to make "eye glass wipers" for spectacles. The instructions for making one type of wiper suggested that two pieces of chamois be cut in the shape of a pansy. The petal outlines were embroidered, then both pieces were buttonhole-stitched together. All work was done with matching silk thread.

Chiffon was a sheer silk fabric used for scarves, blouses, and hat linings. Chiffon dresses covered with laces and embroidery are known, but are extremely scarce now.

Cotton thread was used to make a variety of fabrics including cotton backed satin, canvas, crape that was an imitation of the wool crape, damasks used to make so many towels and tablecloths during this era, calico, cretonne, and cotton ticking. There was also cotton velvet, an imitation of the silk velvet that was so much in demand then, and the plush that was used on mantels and tables—after it was covered with embroidery.

Crape was the simple term used to describe a delicate, transparent crinkled fabric regardless of its content or color. Originally made of silk, crape was later made of wool, then in a cotton and silk combination, and finally of cotton only. The cotton crape was heavier than that made of all silk, but not as heavy as that made entirely of wool.

Crash was the name given to a variety of fabrics, including toweling, Russia crash, Barnsley linen, and huckaback or huck towel-

ing. It was made of either linen or cotton, and sometimes a mixture of the two.

Crepe de Chine was another of the soft silk crepes that was used mainly for a child's or adult's clothing. But as soft and fragile as it seemed to be, it often was covered with embroidery.

Damask fabric was named for the city of Damascus, where it originated before the twelfth century. First it was made of silk, but later it was made of silk mixed with cotton, wool, or linen. Since it had large designs woven in it, it was not considered the best for embroidery by some workers, but was used frequently for monogrammed tablecloths, napkins, and towels. Tatted or crocheted borders and insertions often are found on monogrammed damask towels.

Denim or *blue jean* fabric was and still is a coarse twilled cotton that was first made in Nîmes in southern France. In 1891 several writers on needlework complained of the high cost of plush, velvet, silk, and linen, and suggested that the women should use more of the inexpensive denim. It was used to make such embroidered items as foot pillows, table covers, sewing machine covers, and covers for footstools. One suggested embroidering a blue "crumb cloth" that could be bordered with blue-and-white-striped ticking.

Dimity was a cotton fabric originally imported from the Arab countries. Eventually it was made in America as well as most European countries. This was a favorite for baby clothes, tea aprons, and summer underwear if covered in fine tucks and fancy stitchery.

Doeskin cloth was made in two thicknesses, one slightly heavier than the other. It had a very smooth upper surface and was made to be used as a substitute for the more expensive genuine doeskin.

Egyptian cloth, also called "Momie cloth" because it was made to imitate the fabrics found wrapped around the mummies, was used extensively by embroiderers. It was a heavy cotton fabric that was easy to work and long lasting.

Faille, made with rayon thread, was highly recommended as the perfect material for embroidery after the turn of the century.

Also called rayon faille, it originally was made in France, where it was first made of silk. Wool faille and cotton faille followed.

Felt is a fabric that is not woven but is made by rolling and pressing wool, rabbit fur, hair, and other substances together using high degrees of heat. Later chemicals would be used in the manufacturing processes; but the Tartars simply beat, rolled, and pressed it together to form material used for their clothing and tents. The first felt made in England was very stiff and was used to make hats. Later a soft, pliable felt suitable for embroidery was made in France and eventually in the United States.

Flannel is a word used to describe a specific type of fabric, but it is more closely associated with underwear—red flannels. Originally made of wool to form a soft, fleecy fabric, it was later made of cotton and called *flannelette*. Today only cotton flannel is available except by special order. Around the turn of the century, this was the favorite fabric for making and embroidering parts of the baby layette, especially the long nightgowns. Adults also liked the long embroidered flannel nightgowns and nightshirts.

Georgette was a sheer, transparent, slightly crinkled silk fabric that was named for Parisian modiste Georgette de la Plante. It was used to make scarves, blouses, dresses, and was a favorite for lining children's velvet caps.

Huckaback, shortened to just "huck," was a coarse type of linen woven with small knots at close and regular intervals, giving it a rough texture. Later it was made of a mixture of linen and cotton and finally of cotton alone. It was a favorite among embroiderers when making towels or splashers.

Indian head was a name given a late, heavy woven cotton fabric that apparently originated in the United States. It was used for many household linens during the first part of this century.

Jute was a heavy, coarse cloth made from the silky fibers found under the bark of some plants found growing in China, India, and Ceylon. Around 1845 the fibers began to be shipped to England, where machinery was installed that would make jute by combining the fibers with thread. The fibers were used with cotton, linen, wool, cocoa fibers, and silk to create specific types of jute, some excellent for embroidery.

Kidskin was used to make gloves and slippers. Some gloves and slippers were elaborately embroidered while others might have only a decorative touch of needlework. Kidskin was a leather product made from the skin of young goats who were slaughtered before they were weaned. One idea for using kidskin in needlework was passed on by an old-timer who suggested a case for unanswered letters. Pieces of white kidskin were glued to pieces of cardboard to make a back and front. Before the two pieces were put together a ruffle of blue moire was inserted between the two. Next, the worker embroidered a spray of blue bells and the words "Unanswered Letters" on a piece of white linen that was glued on the front panel. The case then was hung on the wall with blue ribbon.

Leather is the term used to describe the prepared skins of all animals, including goat, sheep, beaver, cow, and buffalo. Some were too heavy for needlework, but much of the lighter, softly tanned leathers were used. Embroidered leather table covers for center tables were made but are difficult to find today. The heavier leathers were used to create a type of cutwork on pillows and accessories. The design was cut, designs were embroidered sparingly, and finally the piece was lined with bright silk. The silk would show through the cut leather and give each piece a different yet effective appearance.

Linen is an all-encompassing term used to describe all fabrics made with flax. Before the invention of factory looms, preparing and spinning flax was a long and tedious chore. The quality of the fabric depended on the texture of the thread. Early settlers wove a heavy, coarse linen with large threads. Like everything else, there were a few skilled spinners and weavers who could turn out fine linen fabric. When the machines took over the weaving, they made some fabric so fine it was called *handkerchief linen*. A damask made of cotton and linen called *linen damask* was the choice for towels, tablecloths, napkins, and splashers.

Linsey-woolsey is thought to have been an

American creation, a coarse woven wool and linen fabric made by the early settlers. That *combination* might be an American creation, but in England the names were used separately to describe two specific types of fabric. Linsey was named for the English town of Linsey in Suffolk where it was made; woolsey, made of cotton and wool, was a different English fabric. Not much embroidery was done on this fabric, although occasionally samplers will be found with a background of linsey-woolsey.

Marquisette was a lightweight, open-mesh fabric made of cotton and silk. It was not among the favorites when it came to embroidery fabrics, but it was used some.

Moire often has been called "watered silk" because of the design. The watered effect resulted from the silk having been pressed in such a manner as to force the air and moisture (of the dampened fabric) through the folds, thereby giving it a circled or wavy look. Moire was used more for clothing than for household linens, but some of the moire clothing was more richly embroidered than the linens. It often was used in combination with other fabrics for making cases, a type of household gadget the Victorian ladies loved. Moire was the fabric used to make the ruffled border on the kidskin case for unanswered letters.

Muslin is probably one of the best known of all cotton fabrics, and was made in a variety of types and grades. Mull muslin was soft and thin, Swiss muslin was a finer grade, and cambric muslin was an imitation of the real cambric. These variations are one of the reasons it is almost impossible now to determine exactly which fabric was used, as some were imitations of others. Muslin is a thin cotton fabric that originated in Mosul, Iraq, from whence it obtained its name. Around 1670 muslin was introduced into England, and by circa 1700 they had begun making their own rather than importing it. The exact date muslin was first made in America is not known, but in 1846 Wamsutta Mills in New Bedford, Massachusetts, was producing thousands of yards annually.

Nainsook was a type of muslin that could be made either plain or with a stripe through it.

A beautiful embroidered bedspread has been found in nainsook with a dainty floral design that was so well done that the back is almost as perfect as the top.

Nankeen was originally a buff-colored cotton fabric made in China. Later it would be made in both America and Europe in white as well as in colors.

Organdy is a sheer, lightweight cotton fabric, rather stiff in the poorer grades, that was used to make blouses, hats, pincushions, curtains, skirts for both vanities and basinettes, and fancy aprons. The fabric, which can only be special-ordered or found in a few specialty shops today, lends itself beautifully to ruffles, fine laces, ribbons, and embroidery. Generally salespeople today will try to substitute a new polyester fabric when the customer asks for organdy. New polyester materials will work in some cases, but they don't have the body of organdy.

Persian lawn was the fabric most often suggested for really fine embroidery in old magazine articles. "Lawn" would suggest a cotton content while "Persian" would indicate that it originated in Persia. It was a fine, closely woven fabric that looked like fine linen.

Pique originated in France. Made of cotton, it was a firmly woven, thicker than usual, fabric with a cord appearance. Although it was made later in the United States, it still retained the French name. This was a favorite fabric for centerpieces and doilies with embroidered centers and crocheted, tatted, or knitted borders.

Pongee was a very soft silk fabric that originated in China or India that was left in its natural beige or tan color. It was used extensively during the first two decades of this century to make lavishly embroidered dresses for both women and children. It would have been almost impossible to hemstitch this fabric by hand, but as soon as machines were available, the embroidered panels in the dresses and blouses were separated by rows and rows of hemstitching.

Poplin, made of silk, wool, or cotton, received its name from having first been made in the papal town of Avignon. The cotton variety was most popular and was used more by the embroiderers.

Sateen was a thick, glossy surfaced cotton fabric made to resemble satin. White sateen was used to make doilies and centerpieces as well as clothing.

Satin was so rich looking and expensive that many imitations were made, including sateen and satinet, both of which were made with cotton rather than silk. Like most fabrics satin was made in different grades and types, and typically was glossy or shiny on top and dull on the bottom. These variations were given names like Satin de Lyons, Royal Satin, and Satin Damask. Since the culture of the silkworm was discovered and developed in China, it was only natural that the Chinese would be the first to create this very desirable silky fabric. In the early days satin was considered a bit more luxurious than regular silk for royal attire.

Silk is another blanket term used to cover all fabrics woven with silk threads. The Chinese originally began weaving the silk fabrics, and as the silkworm culture was introduced into each new country, the weavers there tried to improve on the old methods and create a better fabric. All fabrics made of silk can be described as soft, luxurious, and more expensive than most other types of fabrics. Both a silk damask and a silk serge were made. A special silk canvas was made especially for embroiderers.

Swiss cambric and *Swiss muslin* were two cotton fabrics that were made over a long period of time at Zurich. The cambric was the finer of the two, but today it would be difficult to tell the two apart.

Velvet, with its short and thick nap, is one of the most luxurious fabrics. Italy is credited with being the first country to make excellent silk velvet. Like the other expensive fabrics, it also was made in cheaper grades, and like the others these cheaper versions were a boon to the masses as they could enjoy at least one form of the luxurious velvet. When cotton was mixed with silk in the weaving process, the fabric was called velveteen. There is also a cotton velvet, and this type was the one most commonly used by embroiderers during the past century. It also was used as the canvas or background for numerous oil paintings, an art still practiced in Mexico. Called "painting on velvet," it is a little more difficult than painting on other fabrics. Velvet, silk, and satin were the three fabrics considered fit for a king, and most of their clothing and robes were made of one of these three fabrics.

Voile was a thin sheer fabric made of wool, silk, or cotton, with the latter being the most popular during the decades following the turn of the century. Cotton voile was the fabric most commonly used to make the prestamped, partially made dresses that came in kits. One could choose from many styles and colors (not to mention designs) for clothing that would fit everybody from the toddler to the grandmother. All one had to do was complete the embroidery, do the handwork like whipping on rows and rows of lace, and then she had a garment like hundreds of other people. That was one of the reasons so many talented ladies bought their voile, stamped the dress with an original design, and then embroidered it.

Wool is another blanket term used to cover all fabrics woven with wool threads. Wool could be heavy or light, and, like the silks and cottons, was sold under a variety of names. No doubt, wool-backed satin was made into party dresses for winter parties that were held in those drafty, barnlike old houses of a century ago. The outside satin was luxurious while the wool added some much-needed warmth. There was also a wool matelassé made like the silk matelassé, with its embossed or quilted-looking design.

CHAPTER 6

From Antimacassars to Watchcases

In the beginning fancy stitchery was used to decorate clothing. Then, as Christianity spread throughout the known world, it became a fine art that was practiced mostly in the convents and monasteries for the purpose of making church linens and vestments. During the sixteenth and seventeenth centuries, it began to be used more on clothing, and slowly it began to be used in homes to make covers for both chairs and tables. Embroidered bed hangings came into vogue.

The popularity of laces and embroideries on clothing seems to have risen and fallen about as regularly as the tides but not as rapidly. For decades it would be used profusely, then it would dwindle down to near nonexistence. An example within the memory of most people would be lavishly embroidered centerpieces that were used by older people as late as 1940 and in some instances into the 1950s. By the middle of the 1950s, they had all but disappeared. New tables are bare. If anything is used in the dining room, it is generally plastic place mats.

Another example is the extravagantly hand-embroidered dresses made for little girls in the 1920s and 1930s that slowly devolved to simple "smocked frocks" with a few sprays of flowers embroidered on the little white Peter Pan collars in the 1950s. Children's clothing today has little more than machine stitchery.

Little or no embroidery was used on the clothing of children in America during the first century or so after it was settled, but the children were duly instructed in the art of spinning, weaving, knitting, and embroidery. Although it was difficult to get settled in the New World, some of the English women from middle-class families continued their embroidery here just as they had at home in England. The Indian women who were accustomed to doing all the work in the fields called them "lazy squaws" when they did needlework rather than work in the fields. One early record shows that a "virgin" (the name for an unmarried lady in those days) "spent most of her time save that spent in needlework learning French in religious worship." Apparently the practice of needlework slowed with the move westward but never ceased.

It is believed that the needlework done during those early days was used more on household linens (pictures, chair covers, cushions, bed hangings, and so forth) than on clothing.

Needlework was so important that it was

Exquisite centerpiece with drawn work border and silk thread embroidery surrounding drawn work design in corner.

Round embroidered tablecloth with centerpiece, napkin, and bread basket cover.

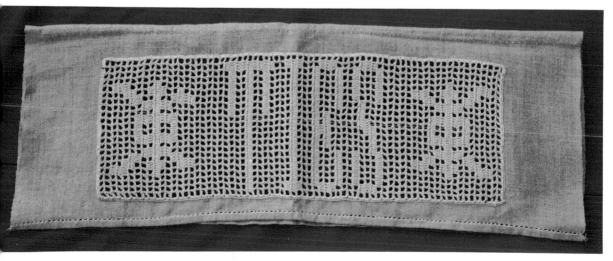

Crocheted case for neckties.

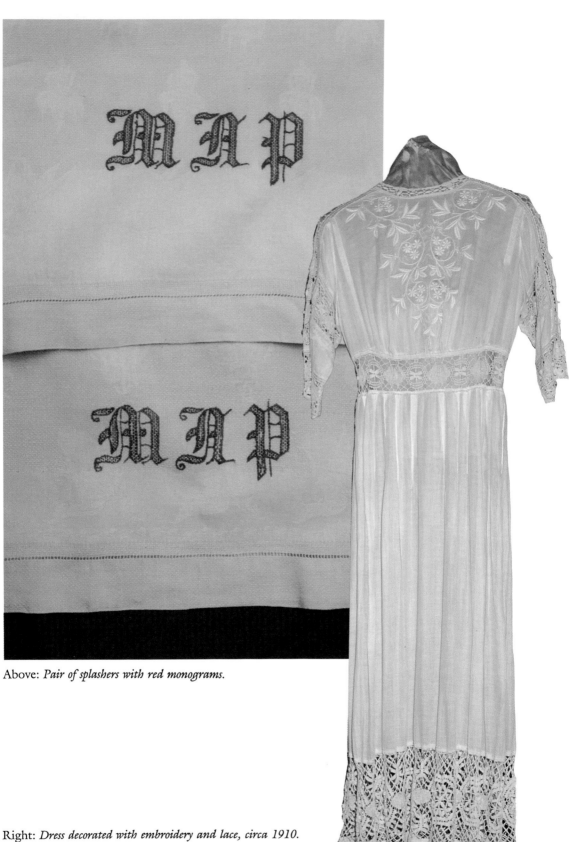

Above: *Pair of splashers with red monograms.*

Right: *Dress decorated with embroidery and lace, circa 1910.*

Altar cloth from a country church.

Doilies embroidered in color, circa 1900.

Right: *Wool-on-wool pillow top, wool embroidery on wool fabric.*

Below: *Crocheted purse.*

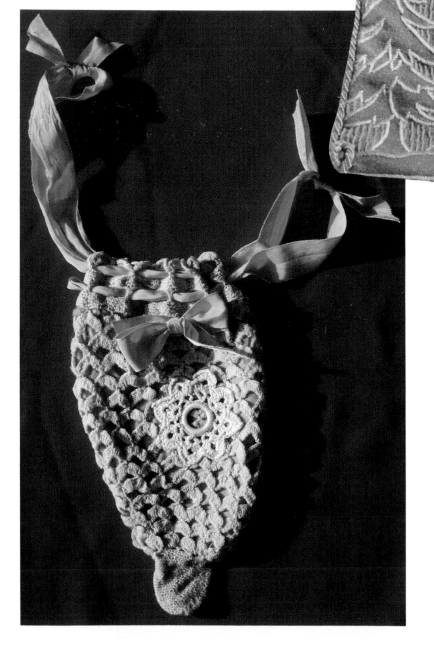

Below: *Embroidered bread basket covers.*

Drawn work centerpiece with different design in
each square.

Bag in colored embroidery, circa 1875.

Top: *Crocheted antimacassars for loveseat.*

Bottom: *Boudoir cap crocheted with blue thread.*

Above: *Three pieces in a combination of crochet and tatting.*

Right: *Blue tablecloth with tatted insertion and corners. Tatted baby cap on top.*

Crocheted door hanging for front doors with a half glass section.

Crocheted key holder, popular in both England and the United States.

Novelty made of pillow lace.

listed in old wills and inventories. It is possible that some of the work was brought with the early settlers when they came to America, but women who enjoyed needlework no doubt continued as long as they lived. Therefore, it would be safe to assume that the wife of the governor of the New Haven Colony (John Winthrop, Jr.) did much of the needlework listed in his 1657 will. Among the special pieces were "an embroidered cubberd cloth [thought to be a cupboard cloth], a turkey carpette [at that time carpets were used as table covers, not floor covers], and a great chaire

During or shortly after the Civil War, the Great Seal of the Confederacy was done in embroidery.

with needleworke." Since most wills and inventories of the more important families of those early days included a cupboard (or as they spelled it "cubberd") as well as one or more cubberd cloths, it would appear the cloth was a necessity. When fabric is mentioned in the old wills and inventories it was either "laced, cambrick, kalliko, needleworke, velvet or simply cloth."

As the years passed, women had more time to spend on their needlework, and they began to make a wider variety of items—some embroidered, others tatted, some made of lace, and others knitted. The trend was developing to combine two or more of the different types of needlework into one item. It would be well into the eighteenth century before household linens as we know them would be made in limited amounts, and then only by the wealthier families living in the cities and towns. It would be nearly another century before they would be made in large quantities in every conceivable fabric and for every conceivable use by the farm wife as well as the society matron.

When small pieces of needlework are found today, collectors are inclined to believe they were made that size by our "waste not, want not" ancestors who refused to throw away even a scrap of fabric. In a few cases this was true, but generally they were made small for a specific purpose. During the last quarter of the nineteenth century, it became fashionable to have doilies for every purpose, and to be socially correct these doilies had to be a specific size for use with certain items. Oftentimes the doilies made for a specific purpose could be used for another purpose that required the same size doily, but these were limited. When making new doilies one always adhered to the accepted size for that particular doily. For instance, the bud vase doily was always exactly seven inches in diameter.

The following list of clothing and household linens may not be complete, but it will give the collector an idea of the variety of items made and hopefully will help to identify pieces when found or those already in the collection. Since clothing was usually worn out or discarded, it is more difficult to find now, but it is known that everything from aprons to veils were made.

The *antimacassar,* also called a tidy, can be found in all shapes and sizes now as they were made in sets of three—a large one for the back of the chair and two smaller ones for either arm. The antimacassars were made to protect the upholstery on the chair, especially the back, where most men rested their heads. In fact, they were named for the hair oil the men used so unstintingly. At one time farm folk could not afford the "store boughten" hair oil, so they substituted bear grease. Regardless of what they used, it was used in large amounts—apparently based on the theory that if a little would help, a lot was bound to hold their hair parted exactly in the middle.

Aprons came in assorted sizes, from the dainty tea apron to the huge work apron, but all were embroidered with some type of design. The maid's snow-white apron might be plain, but it would more than likely have at least one row of crocheted or tatted lace.

The average mother probably spent more time making her first *baby's layette* than she had spent on the linens in her dower or marriage chest. The layette was done in less time because

Vases of pansies decorate this crocheted antimacassar set.

Sometimes the date was crocheted into the piece.

Crocheted "tea" apron, circa 1950.

Crocheted apron, circa 1930.

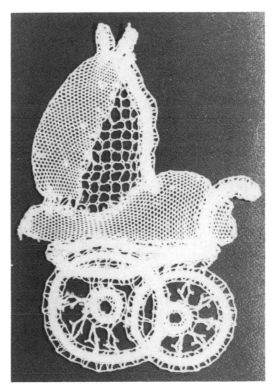

Baby carriage made of pillow lace.

there *was* no surplus time. While she had spent years working on the linens, there were only a few months to complete the layette, so she worked continuously.

If the baby was a girl, the mother never stopped embroidering clothing for her. From the christening dress to the wedding dress, the mother kept plying the needle. For the layette she made dainty little embroidered dresses, slips, bibs, and blankets. Since the baby's head

Yoke of baby dress has drawn work and tucks.

Tatted baby cap with new ribbon rosettes.

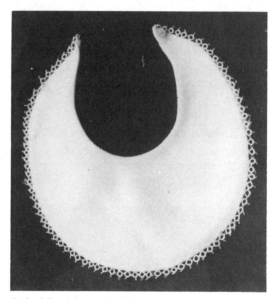

Baby bib with tatted edging.

was nearly always visible, caps were the crowning glory. They could be either tatted; crocheted; knitted; or daintily embroidered on silk, velvet, or the finest linen. Blankets and carriage covers or robes were always embroidered, as was the strap used to hold the cover in place. It was usually a short, beautifully embroidered piece that could be mistaken for a short belt. Gowns were another item on which the mother showed her expertise with the needle. Kimonos and sacques (the latter is a loose jacket with big sleeves) were handy to slip on the baby on cool mornings, so the mother made plenty of them using whatever fabrics were available. Each was embroidered daintily.

Crocheted bedspread on sleigh bed.

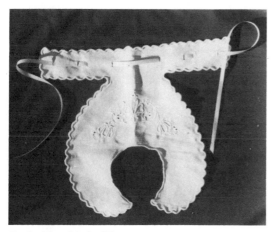

Embroidered baby bib.

Shoes for the baby were another item made by the needle-wielding mother. Not only did she make shoes from scratch, but she also worked the buttonholes for the ribbon ties, made a fancy border around the top, and then embroidered small flowers all over the toes. She also knitted and crocheted bootees for the baby. As the children grew older, they were put in "rompers," a type of playsuit consisting of a shirtwaist and knee-length, banded leg pants with a flared-out space on either hip. These also sported some type of embroidery, usually only a small spray of flowers on the tiny collar and cuffs.

In the early days *bedspreads* often were made of the same fabric as the bed hangings, those curtainlike drapes used around the old beds to keep out the cold air, and were embroidered with the same designs. Later the bedspreads would be made of every known fabric—from hand-loomed wool to sheer batiste—and the majority would be embroidered. Some of the old bedspreads are a combination of appliqué and embroidery while others combine crochet and embroidery. Many will be found made entirely of crochet.

During this time, when it was fashionable to embroider everything, many people kept canaries in cages. In keeping with the trend to embroider everything, they made and embroidered *bird cage covers*. Since the bird had to be covered at night, why not do it fashionably?

The *bookmarker* was another small item that was a favorite of needleworkers. They were easy to make, were nice, inexpensive gifts,

Bookmarks were made by embroidering mottos on perforated paper.

and could be made in a variety of styles—including one where four ribbons of different lengths were attached to a brass ring. Each ribbon had a short phrase or quotation embroidered on it.

In later years the game of bridge became so popular that everybody who played or entertained their bridge clubs had dozens of specially embroidered *bridge table cloths*. They also embroidered covers for the score pads. In addition, they made large embroidered covers for all types of books, including novels, baby books, and brides' books (then called wedding books).

Buttons might be small, but nothing went unnoticed by those skilled embroiderers. They would embroider a small flower or a tiny spray of flowers on fabric that was then used to cover buttons.

They also made *button bags* to hold pearl, brass, ivory and porcelain buttons. They usually were made round in shape, similar to a drawstring bag with cardboard in the bottom to hold the bag in shape.

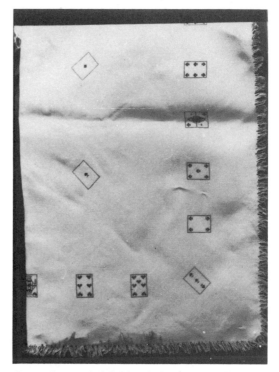

Counted cross-stitch bridge cloth, circa 1940.

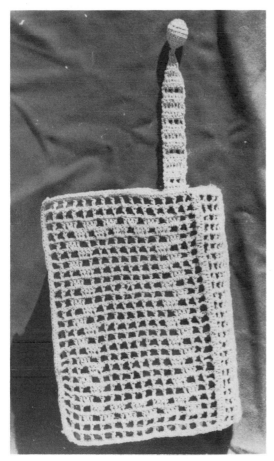

Crocheted cover with bookmark was made for the family Bible.

Handled bag with various types of early embroidery, circa 1875.

Counted cross-stitch design in center of bridge cloth.

The making and embroidering of *bags* and *cases* was overwhelming. They made them to fit everything and every need—from celery to curling irons. There were bags or cases, all beautifully embroidered, to hold nightgowns, cravats, shirts, corsets, shoes, veils, laundry, men's stiff collars, jewelry, handkerchiefs, washcloths, and anything else that could be stuffed into a case. There was a tall, skinny drawstring bag for hatpins with a test tube inside to keep the pins from going through the fabric. Many had the name of the item embroidered on the front. A monogrammed case edged with handmade lace was found on a hot water bottle!

One of the nice things about embroidered *calendars* was the fact that they could be used for years, only the date pad needed to be changed each year. They could be made in any size or shape, and were great for utilizing odd pieces of fabric. All types of florals, from violets

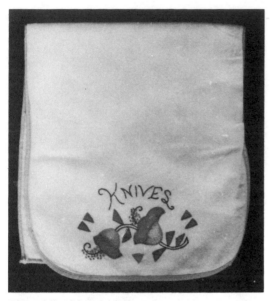

Flannel-lined bag for knives.

Spoon bag in appliqué and embroidery matched the knife and fork bags.

Matching bag for forks.

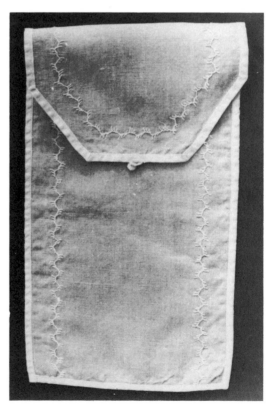

Featherstitched brown linen corset bag.

to roses, were used, as were children and animals. A bit of ribbon could be added so they could be hung on the wall or an easel back could be attached so they would stand on the desk or table. A few of the more elaborate ones were put inside little metal photo frames so they would stand on the desk. Many had verses

Use for this monogrammed case with tatted border is unknown. There is a diagonal opening across one corner of the back.

Although the bag was embroidered, it was made to hold crochet thread.

Bags were made for everything, including darning.

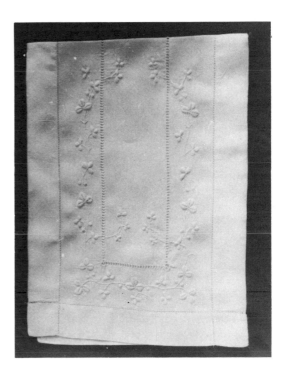

Embroidered dresser scarf.

Eyeglasses case made and embroidered with wool thread.

Handkerchief bag embroidered in France.

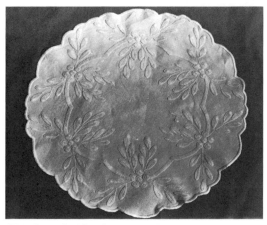

Embroidered centerpiece.

or mottoes. One, apparently done by a disgruntled wife, read, "Not all men are homeless, but some are home less than others."

Centerpieces could be made in any size, shape, and fabric. Many of these combined two or more phases of needlework like the ones with embroidered centers and tatted, knitted, or crocheted borders. The entirely embroidered centerpieces are in the minority; they needed an "edging" of some kind. Their function always has been the same: to cover the center of the table.

Some were made for small tables while others were as large as thirty-six inches in diameter. It was fashionable then to use the large centerpieces on dining room tables. Sometimes they were used alone and other times they were placed over the regular cloth. The only explanation for using both seems to

Heavily embroidered centerpiece.

Close-up of drawn work inside the silk embroidery.

be that the ladies wanted to show off as much of their handiwork as possible. At night and on Sundays, when the family gathered for the big family meal, the centerpiece was removed. If it had been used alone, then the tablecloth had to be put on the table. The centerpieces always were used on the so-called center tables whether they were in the center of the parlor or in the hall, bedrooms, or on sun porches. Table runners were made for long library tables and often were used in pairs (crossed) on the dining table.

In later years the centerpiece and doilies became interchangeable, but in the early years each had a specific function. Then the centerpieces were used on tables only while the doilies were used under things like plates, trays, and vases. The centerpiece used on the dining table generally measured twenty-four to thirty-six inches in diameter, and was called "the between-meal centerpiece." Like all other needlework, the centerpieces and doilies were usually combinations of various types of needlework.

Skilled settlers devised tools and utensils for the farm and home as they needed them; likewise, needleworkers made trinkets and gadgets as necessary to make their work easier. Also like the settler, the needleworker used whatever materials were available. Fancy sterling silver *chatelaines* were made, but the average farm wife could not afford them. She could and did make a substitute that she called a work case or "lady's companion."

One version of this fancy contraption was called a "housewife." It could be made to hang on the wall, hang at the owner's waist, or sit on a table. One that was an open-box type was begun more like a four-leaf clover (four rounded petals went out, one from each side of the base). Short lengths of narrow ribbon were tacked on two sides of the four sections. On the other two the ribbons were sewn across the entire section and then tacked at intervals so scissors, stilleto, and bodkins could be slipped into the loops. Pockets of silk were attached to the other sections to hold thread and other sewing needs. The case was made by covering the cardboard foundation with silk on the outside and linen on the inside. Small sprays of rosebuds were embroidered about on the inside. To form the case the sides could be pulled up and the ribbon tied in small bows at each corner.

It was not unusual in those days for the well-dressed lady to have her *clothing* as well as her accessories embroidered. Pantaloons, drawers, corset covers, chemises, petticoats, dresses, handbags, parasols, hats, and later her teddies (one piece undergarments) were lavishly embroidered. Parasols and hats were accessories that she made sometimes to match a certain outfit, and in some cases they were made on a mix-and-match basis. Since she made each one and the cost was quite small, she could have as many as a dozen of each if she was talented with a needle and a snappy dresser.

The ladies were not only well dressed when they went shopping or visiting, but their at-home clothes—from boudoir caps to handmade house slippers—also showed their abilities as needleworkers. Nightgowns and later pajamas were embroidered, and might also have edgings and insertions of lace,

Fancy lace jabot.

Lace- and tuck-covered lady's dress, circa 1900.

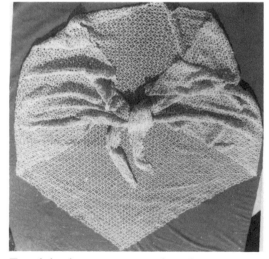

Tatted shawls were worn on cool evenings.

Fancy pair of crocheted gloves.

Crocheted gloves were an essential part of milady's costume well into this century.

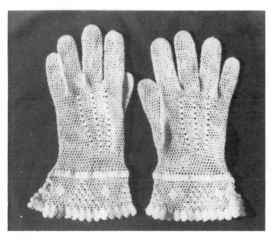

Different-style crocheted summer gloves.

tatting, or crochet. This type of needlework was used on her everyday clothing as well. For those who didn't dress as soon as they were out of bed, there were embroidered robes and kimonos.

During this time, when embroidery was reaching its peak of popularity, nearly all dresses, from the christening dress to mourning attire, were embroidered. Of course the latter was not done as lavishly, and much of it

Dust and boudoir caps were made in many different designs. Note how the ribbon was tied on the back.

was in beading with simple floral designs here and there, but it was all done in black-on-black. After about a year of mourning, the mourners were allowed to cast off the all-black attire and begin to wear a dark gray. These outfits could have a little more embroidery and beading than the black outfits, but it had to be done in gray-on-gray.

This was also an era when embroidered, crocheted, or tatted *collar and cuff sets* were plentiful. They were inexpensive to make since very little material was required, yet they could "dress up" the plainest of dresses. Some were completely covered with embroidery that ranged from all-white to a rainbow of colors on white. Embroidered gifts were considered the nicest presents in a gift-giving era. They were not too expensive and therefore did not create an obligation—except maybe for an embroidered gift in return. Collar and cuff sets were favorites among the gift givers because one size fits all. Embroidered belts were another big favorite. Belts could be made to match the collar and cuff sets or could be made as single items.

Although *curtains* were embroidered, they were not made in as large a volume as other items. Today they are almost extinct. Occasionally, badly worn curtains will be found with a matching bedspread in good condition, so it is believed that the sun proba-

Crocheted gown yoke.

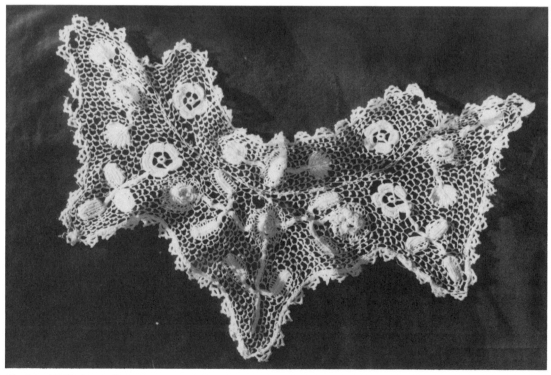

Crocheted Irish lace collar.

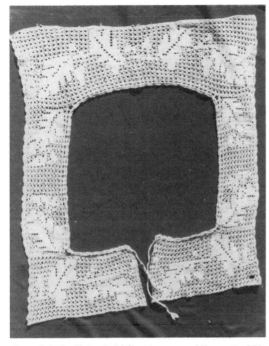

A crocheted collar would fit a square neckline or could be drawn up to fit a round neckline.

Six-by-eight-inch doily, probably made to fit a specific dish.

bly caused the fabric in the curtains to deteriorate long before the bedspread was affected.

Desk sets were a favorite with embroiderers. Along with shirt cases, collar bags, and cigar cases, this was about the only embroidered piece men tolerated. The desk set usually included a desk pad, a blotter bordered with a strip of embroidered fabric, and a matching embroidered calendar. Sometimes a photo frame embroidered to match the rest of the set was included.

The *doily* was named for a seventeenth-century draper and merchant named Doily or Doyley who sold cloth and dry goods. The name has been found spelled both ways. Few people can claim their name was used as frequently as Mr. Doily, as the amount of doilies made in this country was staggering. Their uses were as varied as their sizes, but generally the size will determine the use for which it was created. Of course the same size was used for different purposes in a few instances, so unless the history is known, it will be difficult to place each and every one in a specific category.

Embroidered doily.

Hopefully the measurements used by the late nineteenth-century needleworkers will be helpful in sorting doilies according to use, but some confusion is bound to arise when trying to differentiate between a twelve-inch doily and a twelve-inch centerpiece. About the only

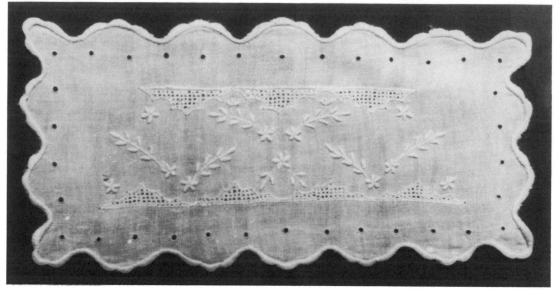

Embroidered bread tray doily.

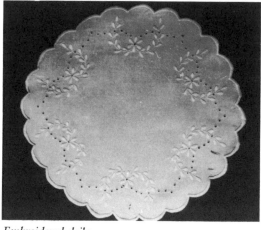

Embroidered doily.

Small doily with crocheted border and drawn work center.

way to be absolutely certain is to know the history. If there is more than one exactly alike, there can be little doubt that they are doilies.

At that time custom decreed the service-plate doily be exactly twelve inches in diameter. That was also a popular size for small centerpieces. Another one that could be confusing is the sixteen-inch doily that was made especially for lamps. Centerpieces also were made in that size as well as the eighteen-inch ones that were made later for the electroliers,

those fancy new glass table lamps with large glass shades. There is no set rule for distinguishing between them except the sizes, and it really isn't essential as most of today's collectors are more interested in the workmanship than in the original use.

For those times when tablecloths were not used, doilies were made to be used under

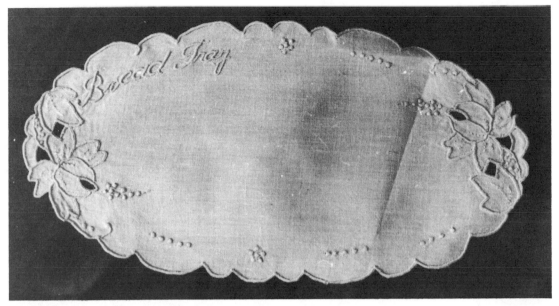

Bread tray doily.

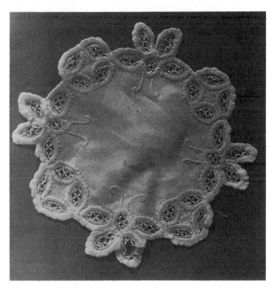

Rose bowl doily.

Rose bowl doily with tatted border.

each piece of the place setting. The correct size for the bread and butter plate doily was eight inches. No mention is made of a saucer doily, but the cup required a four-inch doily. Now whether this was a substitute for the old cup plate or was to be used between the cup and saucer is unknown. Three doilies, for the frappé, bullion, and finger bowl, were all the same size—seven inches. The correct size for the water set doilies was ten inches for the pitcher and five inches for each tumbler. Carafe doilies could be either nine or eleven inches depending on the size of the base. The doily for the oblong celery tray was supposed to be nine-by-fifteen inches while the one for the bread tray was made eleven-by-sixteen inches. When a doily was made for the bonbon tray it always

Embroidered cloth for meat tray or platter.

Library table scarf with crocheted monograms on either end.

measured nine-by-twelve inches. The olive dish, usually made of cut glass (if one could afford it), was ten inches in diameter. Since most olive dishes were seldom over five or six inches in diameter, this extra size raises some question as to why the increase was needed. After all, the doily for a rose bowl was only nine inches. There was a tray or carving cloth, usually with a carving set embroidered on it that was designed to be placed under the large

One part of a three-piece vanity set.

Library table scarf embroidered in red.

platters to protect the table. No specific size was given for the carving cloth, as the maker knew to make it a size larger than her own platter.

The doilies for place settings and water sets were used only when a meal or tea was served on a table without a cloth. It was suggested that the doilies could serve a dual role: When they were not in use on the table, they could be placed on the shelves of china cabinets and cupboards to show the china and glass stored in them to better advantage. Again the doilies could be done entirely in embroidery, entirely in crochet, or a combination of both.

Those long runners that resembled table runners, except for the fact that they were shorter and not nearly as wide, were called *dresser scarves*. They were used on dressers and chests as well as on washstands. The ladies often made several matching dresser scarves so they could be used on all the pieces of furniture in the room. Like all the other household linens, they could be embroidered, crocheted, tatted, knitted, or a combination.

To better understand the way needlework was used during this period, it is necessary to understand household furnishings. It also is essential to realize that each person had his or her own preference and that each room in the house was a reflection of its owner and his or her likes and dislikes. Most of the well-to-do wives read the current magazines and tried to do everything that fashion and custom decreed.

Many fashion followers must have been in a turmoil after a distinguished interior decorator wrote in one of the better magazines in 1890 that "The most tastefully arranged parlor now has no two pieces of furniture alike; but two easy chairs placed opposite each other are never out of place. Here may stand an embroidered ottoman, there a quaint little chair, a divan can take some central position, a cottage piano covered with some embroidery may stand at one end of the room while an ebony or mahogany cabinet with its panel mirrors and quaint brasses may be placed at the other end, its racks and shelves affording an elegant display of pretty pieces of bric-a-brac." Use of

Fringed shelf cloth with red embroidery.

more embroidered pieces were suggested, with "a scarf or sash of bright embroidered plush or silk flung over a table, the ends drooping very low," and the mantle covered with a "corresponding piece."

The *fire screen* was yet another place where the skilled embroiderer could show off her talents. Some of those old houses had as many as a dozen fireplaces, making each room a stage on which to display her work. Most of the screens were different.

One that was very popular around 1900 had a design of huge chrysanthemums done in pink and yellow on black satin. When using satin on the fire screens, the fabric required special preparation. First, a strong muslin was stretched on the embroidery frame and covered with a thin paste rubbed well into the fabric. Care had to be taken to see that no small lumps of the paste were left on the muslin. As soon as the paste was smooth, the satin was placed over it and covered with a folded sheet.

When the paste had dried thoroughly, the embroidery could "commence and the work proceed as usual." Once the embroidery was completed, another batch of paste was rubbed on the back.

A piece of satin, usually in a color that matched one of the embroidery colors, was attached to the back side. This covered the stitches on the back and made it reversible if one decided they preferred the side without embroidery. When the last drying process was completed, the screen was removed from the embroidery frame and mounted in or on the fire screen frame.

Handkerchiefs were known as early as the fifteenth century, because records of Edward IV show that he had a dozen at one time. Unfortunately there is no record of the sizes, styles, or types that were used at that time. During the next few centuries the handkerchief would be used as a covering for women's heads, and later to be sniffed at then

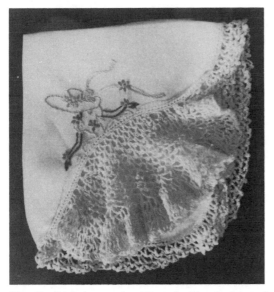

Handkerchief decorated with embroidered girl and crocheted hoop skirt.

tucked into the man's coat sleeve. The woman kept theirs in their hands so they could sniff into them, wave them, and in general show off their handiwork.

Then handkerchiefs became so commonplace and were used so universally that everyone carried a "hankie" whenever they went out. This custom made it easy for young people—even though they were carefully chaperoned—to work out a system of signals that enabled them to carry on a conversation across the room. For instance, if the young lady drew the handkerchief across her lips while looking at a young man, it meant she "was desirous of making his acquaintance." If she already knew the young man, signals could get personal. For example, when she drew the handkerchief across her cheek, it meant "I love you." If the hankie was held to the right cheek it meant "yes" while on the left cheek it meant "no." When it was drawn across the forehead it meant "we are being watched," but when it was thrown over her shoulder it meant "follow me." It is not unusual at all to find all these old handkerchief signals written in beautiful script on yellowing paper tucked away in the bottom of an old handkerchief box. Some handkerchiefs were made completely of lace, others were embroidered and edged in lace, and a good amount only had tatted borders. Handkerchiefs were considered the perfect gift for everyone, including mere acquaintances. Hence, they were made and exchanged by the thousands.

Hatpin holders were made exactly like regular pincushions except they were thicker. This type was used on the dresser; there also was the tall, skinny handbag variety with the test tube in the center to hold the hatpins. The drawstring top allowed it to be hung when used at home and closed for traveling. This was a time when ladies wore large, broad-brimmed hats, and hatpins were essential to keep them on.

Instructions for making *linings for chiffonier drawers* are shown in at least one old needlework magazine. It would be natural to assume that if they were made for chiffoniers they also were made for the drawers of dressers, chests, and washstands. According to the instructions they were made to fit the specific drawer. The center was embroidered with a nice floral design while the edges were finished with a blanket stitch or narrow tatted or crocheted lace.

Liners for comb and brush trays also were made to fit the specific tray, and could be either oblong, oval, or round. The embroidered liner was done in an elegant design so it could be shown to advantage under the glass on the tray.

Match scratchers were an area of needlework where the embroiderer could show a sense of humor. Usually made of a square, sturdy fabric with a piece of sandpaper attached for the actual scratching or striking, match scratchers would have funny characters and matching slogans. On one of the most humorous pieces, the worker had embroidered the back view of a very stout man and attached the sandpaper to his posterior. Embroidered down the side was "Don't scratch matches on the wall, scratch them on my overalls." This was a time when oil lamps had to be lighted and fires were started with matches, so the match scratcher was another essential item—unless you scratched matches on the wall.

In early times women not only didn't have much money, but they also didn't have a purse

Embroidered folder for napkins.

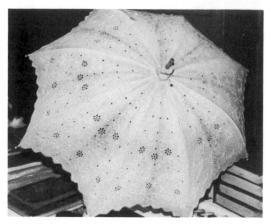

Parasol with embroidered cover.

Embroidered picture frame.

or handbag in which to carry their money. But they were ingenious souls, and in order to protect what little money they did have, they kept it with them at all times in an elaborately embroidered *money bag* made of chamois that was worn around the neck.

Most *napkin rings* were crocheted, but now and then some industrious embroider would make a dozen or so with scalloped, buttonholed edges. A few tiny flowers would be embroidered around the ring with a buttonhole and button on top to allow the ring to be opened for easy ironing and closed for use.

Needle cases could be made of any fabric and in any size, but the center always was made of flannel. Needles were expensive, so they were stored carefully. But even with the best of care, needles occasionally would develop rough or rusty spots. For that reason many needle cases or needle books had an emery attached. The needles could be run through the emery and the rust would disappear. Poorer people found a substitute for the emery: they held the rusty needle between their thumbs and forefinger and rubbed it through their long hair. Small needle cases, those made like a book with a piece of flannel in the center, were the large roll types that held several packages of needles, an emery, and possibly a needle threader. Regardless of the size, most needle cases were embroidered.

Parasols were almost as important to the Victorian ladies as their handkerchiefs. Whether they were simply going for a stroll, to visit a friend, or shopping, they carried a parasol for looks and to use. Parasols protected them from the sun as this was a time when a creamy, white complexion was their most treasured possession. Once they found they could embroider the covers to match any outfit or ones that were interchangeable, the race was on to see how many could be made. Like everything else, when the fad had passed the parasols were sent to the attic to rot.

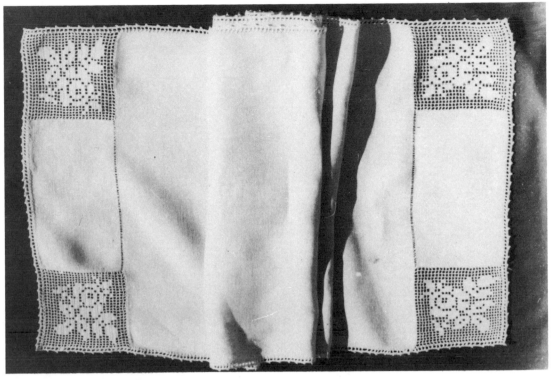

Piano scarf with crocheted floral corners.

Pen wipers could be made individually or as part of the desk set. In those days all writing was done with a pen that was dipped in an inkwell at regular intervals. Once the writing was completed, the ink had to be wiped from the pen point before it was laid on the rack. For this chore one needed a pen wiper. One of the prettiest pen wipers was made by cutting five petals; the three smaller petals used on the bottom were cut from yellow satin while the larger two that would form the top were cut from purple velvet. A small hem was turned up on each piece and fastened with a buttonhole stitch using thread of the same color as that of the fabric. The pieces then were tacked together to form a pansy blossom. A few rows of outline stitches were worked around the center to resemble the stamen. Two pieces of chamois used for the actual pen wiping were cut in the exact size of the blossom and tacked on the back.

Piano scarves usually were square and lavishly embroidered, then draped over grand pianos. For an upright piano the scarf was a long runner type that resembled the table run-

ner. Battenberg cloths often were made for the upright. Seldom if ever were they made completely in crochet, knitting, or tatting. Frequently edging made by one of these methods was used on an embroidered scarf.

Picture and photo frames were another favorite of the needleworker. They were made in singles, pairs, and as part of desk sets. The design was embroidered on the fabric that was then glued to a piece of cardboard that already had been cut to size. A stronger piece was attached to the back and the frame could be hung with ribbon on the wall or with an easel-type back could stand on the desk or table.

Pillowcases and *pillow shams* were elaborately embroidered. During the Civil War era and for a while afterwards it was the custom to have several goose down pillows on the bed and at least two propped up against the solid headboard. These were lavishly embroidered and would have wide embroidered ruffles around them. Apparently the trend then was to use white on white. Later the cases and shams would be embroidered in colors with various messages, like "Sweet lilies close their leaves at

Small embroidered picture frame.

Pillow top with colored embroidery, circa 1910.

Monogrammed and embroidered napkins aren't as popular as they once were, but they still can be used to make beautiful throw pillows.

Embroidered cover for a picture album.

night" on one side and "And opens with the morning light" on the other. Many had "Good Night" on one case and "Good Morning" on the other; one pair had "I slept and dreamed that life was beauty" on one sham and the surprising message "I awoke to find it was a life of duty" on the other. Along with the messages were large sprays of flowers embroidered in living color.

Pincushions ran the gamut from small, frilly, organdy cushions to large plain ones, but all were embroidered. Some might have just a small spray of flowers or a rosebud here and there while others might have the top done solidly in elaborate embroidery. Some were decorated with beading, and some had crocheted, tatted, or knitted tops.

Purses or *pocketbooks* emerged as a necessary accessory for the well-dressed woman during the nineteenth century. The ready-made ones were small and plain. Ladies found they could have original designs as well as ones that matched their outfits if they made the purses themselves. For the cost of one ready-made purse, they could buy enough fabric and thread to make several.

Perhaps the most important factor in

Crocheted pillow shams were popular during the early part of this century.

One of a pair of pillowcases with cross-stitched cat design and crocheted edging.

making their own purses and pocketbooks was the fact that they could create something just a little different than that made by their friends. The most popular purse at that time was one crocheted with beads, but many embroidered ones were made, especially white summer bags. At first, they were all made in the draw-string style, but envelope styles with cardboard liners were made later. The flaps on these were embroidered, and as time progressed more

67

English-style pillow sham embroidered in turkey red chain stitch.

Pillow sham done in turkey red embroidery.

Hanging-type beaded pincushion.

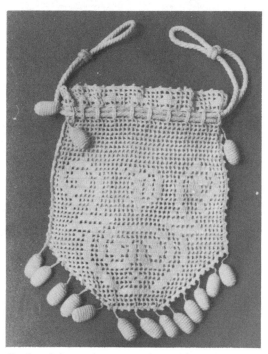

Crocheted drawstring purse, circa 1890.

machine embroidery was found on the purses than hand embroidery.

As we have said, the ladies culled nothing that could not be embroidered. They even made and embroidered pipe racks for the men. Like all needlework, the maker had a choice in the style, design, and shape of the pipe racks, but the majority were oval. One favorite design had two old gentlemen, one on either side, lighting their pipes. "Old Friends" was embroidered in the space between them. When the embroidery was completed, the fabric was ironed, glued onto the cardboard back, and the copper pipe rack attached.

Quilts were made to form optical illusions.

Quilts were the one place where the embroiderer could let her imagination absolutely run wild. Seldom did the old-timers have a stamped design or even a design sketched on the quilt. After they had featherstitched the seams, they made freehand designs. Some were all in satin stitch done with silk thread and others were done in a design that could best be described as a combination of many stitches done with the same twisted thread that was used to do the feather stitching.

Sachets were another small item that was made from the scraps left over from other projects. Fabric was not too plentiful so they saved every little scrap. Many women didn't have the money to buy large amounts of fabric, and these people had been taught from birth not to waste anything. When they wanted to make a small item, they just delved into the old scrap sack until they found something that

Unusual design appliquéd quilt.

69

Appliquéd quilt with another design formed by the fine quilting.

Crazy quilt made with scraps of velvet featherstitched together, and embroidered designs on the larger pieces.

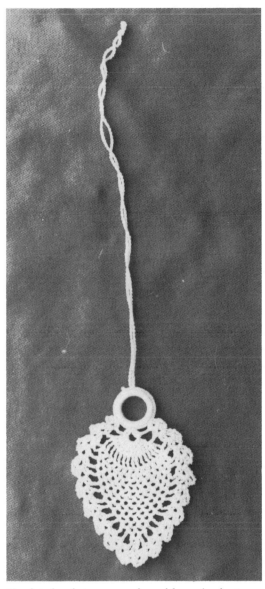

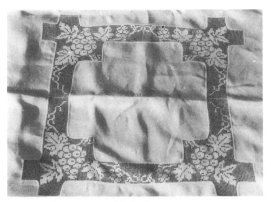

Crocheted center in tablecloth.

Heavily embroidered round tablecloth.

Crocheted sachets were made and hung in closets.

would fit the need. The sachets were filled with rose petals from the potpourri jar or some other scent easily obtained. Sizes varied according to the amount of fabric available, and they could be plain and simple or very elegant.

In this era when everything was covered with a snowy white cloth, it was unthinkable for the sewing machine to be left uncovered. Some used an embroidered runner-type cloth while others made a hood type to fit over the top and partially cover the drawers and base.

The picture made by Dame Brewster was the first piece of embroidery made in America. What the second piece was is unknown. We know that in America the "cubberd cloth" was made early, but more than likely the second piece was a *tablecloth* or a "board cloth" as they were known then. In the early days the table where the family dined, and in some cases the only table in the house, was called the "board." Therefore, the cloth used on it was called a "board cloth." For a time the table coverings were called table-clothes and finally they became known as tablecloths.

As early as 1650 tablecloths were mentioned in wills and inventories of the wealthier colonists. One listed in a 1654 will was described as "enriched with embroidery in colors." Apparently all the upper-class colonists had plenty of napkins at that time, as one inventory listed "two wrought napkins with no lace around them," another listed "half a duzzen [sic] napkins wrought about and laced," while another had two dozen napkins of "layd worke." We can only guess the "wrought" was drawn work and the "layd worke" was embroidery. The wife of the poorest settler soon found that a pretty embroidered tablecloth would enhance a table even if it was set with wooden trenchers (plates) and mugs. As soon as she could weave a piece of fabric that was not essential for other purposes, she made a tablecloth and embroidered it in bright, cheerful colors.

Tablecloths could be round, oblong, or square depending on the shape of the table, but the majority were embroidered. They could be as small as one square yard to fit a bridge table or they could be long enough to cover a banquet table. Some might have only a monogram on each corner while others were completely embroidered. Seldom was there a small tablecloth that was tatted, although some were done entirely in crochet. Some were made with squares of embroidery and squares of crochet assembled to make a large cloth. Table runners were no more than half a yard wide, but they could be any length. They often were used in pairs that were crossed on the smaller tables to make a place for four table settings.

Later custom or fashion decreed that table runners or doilies should be used for breakfast, lunch, and tea while the large tablecloth only would be used for dinner, the evening meal, parties, and family gatherings.

Tie racks were made in a similar fashion to the pipe racks—they were embroidered, glued on cardboard, and then the tie bar was attached. Small rings affixed to the top were used for hanging the tie rack.

Towels and *splashers* were almost identical except for their use. Towels were used everywhere. Splashers were used only on or over the backs of washstands to prevent the wallpaper

Drawn work tea-table cloth.

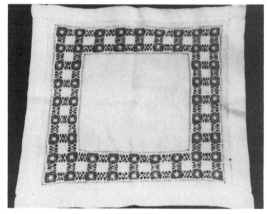

Small tablecloth with drawn work border.

from being splashed while the person washed their hands in the bowl and pitcher on the washstand. Splashers were generally made in one size only: twenty-by-thirty inches. On the other hand, towels were made in a variety of sizes that varied from fourteen-by-twenty-one inches up to seventeen-by-sixty inches. Most were made with monograms or drawn work on either or both ends. Some had insertions of crocheted or tatted lace.

Towel racks were made exactly like the tie racks except that they were a little larger in size and usually had a different type of decoration. The tie rack would be made in a dark-colored fabric (blue was the favorite color) and an embroidered geometric design. The towel rack often was made in white with a floral design.

Corner of an embroidered tea-table cloth.

Fringed towel embroidered in brown thread.

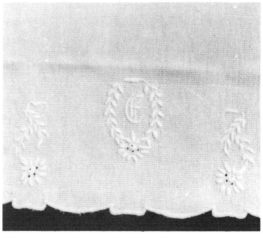

Monogrammed and embroidered towel.

In 1900 the *veil case* was no longer considered a luxury as it had become an "absolute necessity as one might have to wear a point lace veil for one function, a Shetland for another, and an embroidered chiffon for still another" all in one day. Veil cases came in various sizes

Close-up showing drawn work and monogram on splasher.

depending on the size of the veil. Most were elaborately embroidered.

These small cases were considered excellent gifts for friends and family. All small embroidered gifts were appreciated by the recipient, who accepted them as they were given—as tokens of friendship and love.

When the Victrola (phonograph) made its appearance, the ladies weren't about to let it sit around bare. They immediately began designing covers they called *Victrola scarves*. They were either made in the runner or the hood type, but they would be embroidered. By this time much colored embroidery was being done, so many Victrola scarves will be found done in colors.

Since nothing escaped the ladies' embroidery needles, it was only natural that *wastebasket covers* would be handmade and embroidered. A few are known to have been made of expensive linen and profusely embroidered.

During the Victorian era both men and women had gold watches. The lady's watch

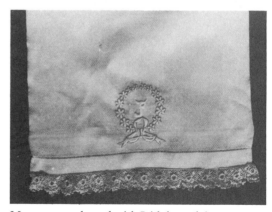

Monogrammed towel with Irish lace edging.

was a hunting case type that was worn around the neck on a long gold chain. The man's watch could be a hunting case or an open face, but regardless of the type worn by either, there was a fancy *watchcase* to hold the watch when it wasn't being worn. Cases were made in two styles: the watch holder (or case) and the watch

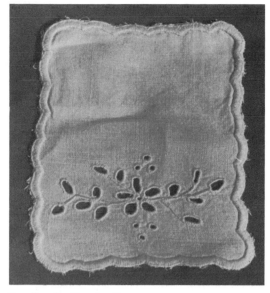

Small embroidered veil case.

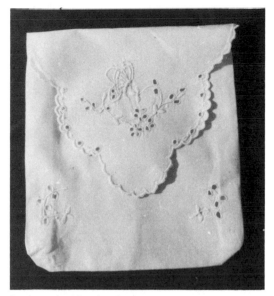

Large embroidered veil case.

stand. The most popular design for the wall watchcase was made by embroidering fabric that would eventually be shaped like the sole and toe of a shoe. Both pieces were attached to cardboard backs in the same shapes, then the toe section was blanket-stitched into place. The toe section was made to fit the watch.

The watch stand was exactly what the name implies. It was used more as a decorative piece on a table or chest than as a case although the watch was kept on it when not being worn.

The design was usually a circle of flowers, open on the top, and embroidered on a small square of linen. When the embroidery was completed the fabric was glued on a square piece of cardboard. A slightly smaller cardboard piece with an easel back was glued to the front piece. A small hook was fastened in the top section of the design. The watch was hung on the hook so that it appeared to be framed by the circle of embroidery.

CHAPTER 7

Types of Embroidery

The names of embroidery stitches may vary from one place to another, and some might be different because someone added an extra stitch here and there, but basically embroidery is the same all over the world and it is done in every country in the world. Few people were born skilled embroiderers. Having some talent is an advantage, but even then embroiderers must be taught to do the work correctly and a great deal of patience is required.

Young children were sent to the convents at an early age on the theory that young minds grasp things more quickly. With enough practice anybody can embroider—whether or not they do beautiful embroidery or not is another story. There were embroiderers who not only were very skilled, but who also would work

Roses were a favorite flower among embroiderers.

Morning glories required less shading than roses.

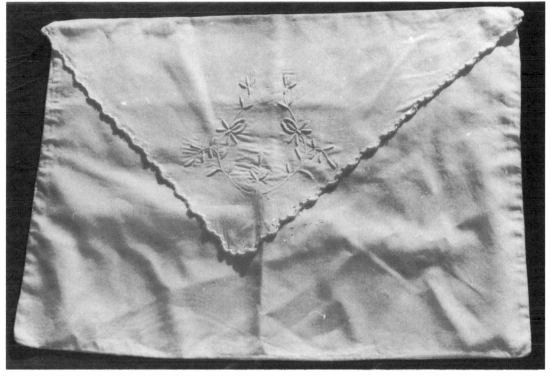

Envelope pillow sham with white on white embroidery.

unceasingly until the work was done perfectly. They would take out stitches that weren't correct and redo them, a time-consuming chore. It is the work that was done by those perfectionists that is the most sought after today, and it commands the highest prices.

Then there were those who created embroidery simply because it was the fashionable thing to do. Much of their work was poorly done and will be priced lower in the marketplace.

When buying an embroidered piece or any type of needlework, examine it carefully for worn places and for overall quality of workmanship. Poor workmanship and worn places should have a great bearing on the price. In fact, checking the price tag is one of the best ways to get an idea of the quality of a piece of needlework before picking it up. Generally the dealer in antique household linens and clothing knows quality fabric and workmanship and will therefore price accordingly.

Of course, bargains, like beauty, are in the eyes of the beholder. When the price seems too good to be true, however, examine the piece extremely carefully. But don't pass up the worn or slightly torn pieces (that are basically good but have a couple of holes or a slight break in the edging) if the price is right and you are skilled with the needle. Talented embroiderers buy quality pieces that aren't quite perfect and then repair them. This way they can have the best at a reasonable price.

Collectors today are not apt to find much of the pre-Victorian era embroidery. The majority of the needlework found now was made during the Victorian era, a time when every lady who could hold a needle was embroidering something. Although not all of it is good, we should still be grateful they made so much because of the wide variety from which to choose.

The Victorian era was basically no different from any other period in history. It was a time when the housewife did not go out to work unless poverty forced her to work in the mills. There were few exceptions. In the socially conscious middle and upper classes, sta-

Small towel with white embroidery.

So many towels were done in different designs that the choice today is almost limitless.

tus was as important if not more important then than it is today. Status largely was dependent on how well the stay-at-home wife maintained her home, how it was furnished, and whether or not she had a generous supply of snow-white household linens done in exqui-

site needlework. There were a few housewives who were not skilled enough to make the fine linens, but they usually were wealthy enough to buy some of the best from their more-talented friends.

The types of embroidery used on clothing

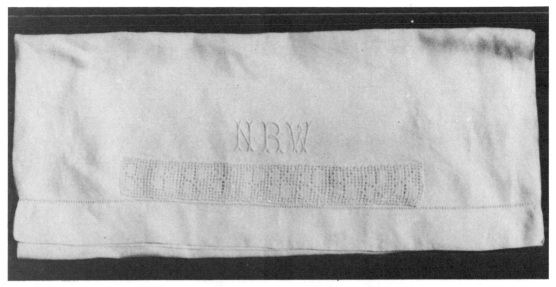

Monogrammed towel with crocheted insertion.

One of a set of finger bowl doilies.

Cozies were made for biscuits, hot rolls, and bread with the name of the bread embroidered in one corner.

Carving tray or platter cloth with well-worn fringe.

changed little unless the styles changed. For more than twenty-five years (1875–1900) the dresses were long and heavily embroidered. Then they began to be made of lighter fabrics and have less embroidery. They also were growing shorter. The dress styles changed considerably during the Roaring Twenties, when the flappers took over with knee-length dresses. These were short, sheer, and could be covered with embroidery, ruffles, beading, feathers, or a combination of several of these. Due to the change in fabric, the embroidery

Embroidered towel with crocheted edging.

was done with finer thread, which gave it a lighter look. The 1930s saw embroidered dresses for ladies practically go out of style. Children's clothing styles also were changing. Where once the entire dress would have been covered with embroidery, now there were a few rosebuds on the little white "Peter Pan" collars and cuffs. This trend, along with smocking on children's dresses, continued on a small scale into the 1950s.

The progression in both dress styles and the types of embroidery used on them was a welcome change for the ladies. They were delighted with changes because the repetitive styles became boring.

In an effort to liven things up a bit and keep the interest of the subscribers, magazines devoted entirely to needlework began naming different types of embroidery. A combination of stitches could replace the former custom of doing that particular design in one single type of stitch. Often these changes were touted as new designs from another country that only recently had been introduced here. In those days the average person seldom thought of traveling across two states in America, much less of going abroad. But they were vitally

Panel from badly damaged blouse showing embroidery combined with lace insertion.

interested in everything that went on "across the waters." After all, Paris was the fashion capital of the world, and the ladies were very interested in the newest fashions even if they couldn't always afford them. Therefore, when

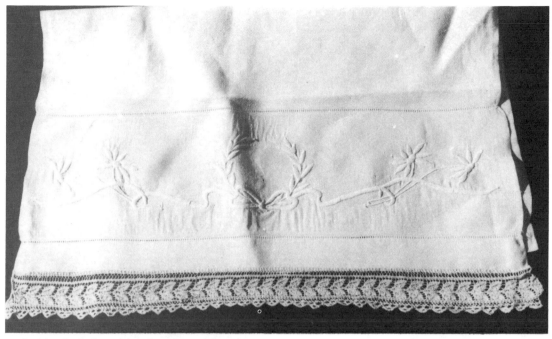

Embroidered splasher with knitted lace edging.

One of a pair of embroidered pillowcases with crocheted edging, circa 1940.

a new type of embroidery was introduced—especially one from another country—the ladies began working with renewed vigor.

As we have said, it is almost impossible in some cases to differentiate between the various types of embroidery or to date them to one specific period. *Berlin* embroidery is a prime example. Although it was not known by that name, the tent and cross-stitches that are the predominate stitches in old Berlin work were used on the early church vestments and linens. When it began to be done on canvas, it became

Pillowcases done in colors with crocheted edging, circa 1940.

The design was printed in colors and then embroidered in this pillow top, circa 1930.

Ten-inch doily that could have had several uses.

known as canvas work or canvas embroidery, and still was used to make cushions and kneelers for the church.

Then circa 1829 a type of wool called Berlin wool was introduced to use on the canvas rather than the silks, crewels, and lamb's wool thread that had formerly been used. This work became known as Berlin work or embroidery. The coarser Berlin wool did not work well on the canvas the embroiderers had been using, so canvas with large holes or openings had to be made. This in turn made the designs larger and less intricate. During the Victorian era other stitches were added to make the Berlin embroidery emerge as yet another type of beautiful embroidery.

Chances of the average person finding a piece of old *bullion* embroidery are extremely remote. This was the name given the very early

Unusual pillow cover embroidered with wool thread on a wool background. Vertical lines of embroidery were used to form a more-pronounced background.

Hardanger-embroidered doily.

Hardanger-embroidered centerpiece.

embroidery that was done using gold wires and gold spangles. Not only was it a very early embroidery, but it also was extremely difficult to do, which limited the amount produced. It was made by couching small wires onto the fabric in an intricate design. If larger wires with holes in the center were used, they were sewn directly to the fabric.

The early Canadian natives were so skilled in quill embroidery that the type of work they did just naturally became known as *Canadian* embroidery. They also were well known for their work with reptile and animal skins. Like the quills, the skins were cut in very small pieces before they were appliquéd to the fabric. The small pieces formed the design. They did

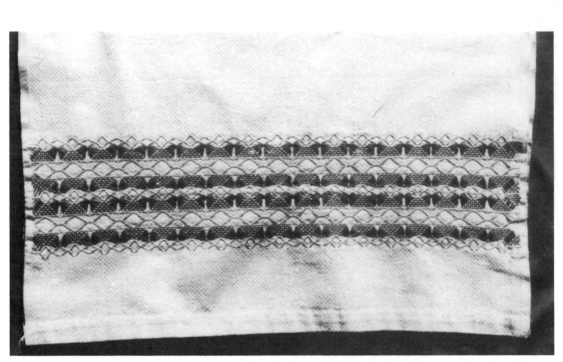

Shortly after the turn of the century, a new type of embroidery called Swedish embroidery was introduced here.

some work with the larger pieces of porcupine quills, but the most desirable work was done with pieces of quill that had been cut so fine that they were used like thread. The work became so popular in the United States that ads in magazines around 1890 offered porcupine quills cut and ready to be used in embroidery. According to the ads, the quills were prepared in Canada by Canadians. The quills were dyed various colors so they could be used to embroider any design, including florals.

We tend to associate the word *chenille,* which is French for "caterpillar," with the tufted bedspreads made during the 1930s, but in grandmother's day it was a type of embroidery. The name was derived from the type of thread used to do the work—a soft fluffy thread that looked somewhat like a big fat caterpillar. When the work was done in satin stitch, it looked even fluffier. Another type of chenille embroidery was done on gold- and silver-perforated cardboard using a tent stitch. It was very attractive. Turn-of-the-century embroiderers loved the elegant look of embroidered silks and satins. One of their favorites was to embroider intricate designs on thin

Porcupine quill embroidery on birchbark box. Quills were dyed to form the designs.

silks, satins, and velvets using chenille embroidery.

Since the Chinese were the first to have the patience to unwind the silkworm cocoons and weave fabric from the thread, it was only

84

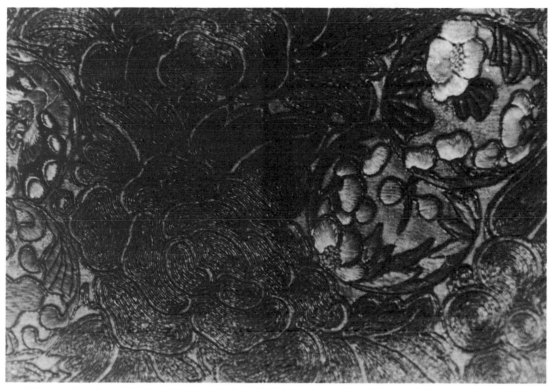

In Chinese embroidery gold thread was couched on silk fabric woven with a different design.

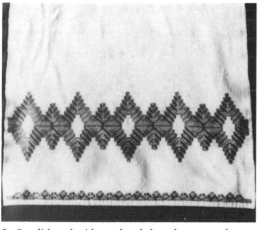

In Swedish embroidery colored threads were used on top of huck fabric to create a design.

natural they would be the ones to create exquisite, intricate embroidery. They are famous for their *Chinese* satin stitch embroidery done with silk thread on silk fabric that is so fine on both sides it is impossible to tell one from the other.

China is one country where there were approximately as many men embroidering as women. Most of their work was done on robes, screens, curtains, and dresses. Until the later years, when they began exporting needlework to other countries, most of their work was confined to their clothing. It was not unusual for them to completely cover the garment with fine embroidery. There is no comparison between the garments they made for themselves and those made for export. Like everything else they exported, the embroidery was very ornate, with large designs in brightly colored threads and average workmanship. They thought Westerners wanted ornate work, and apparently they were correct. They kept the intricate embroidery done in small designs in subdued colors. Their embroidery designs were much like their ceramic designs. They used dragons in large numbers, bats, birds, butterflies, and flowers (usually asters and cherry blossoms). They also used urns and jars in much of their embroidery. Often the flowers

Satin stitch done in silk thread was also a favorite of the Chinese and Japanese.

would appear to have been arranged in the urns, making them look even more realistic.

The term *church* embroidery can be used to cover a multitude of pieces—from the old vestments and linens made by the nuns and their workers in the convents centuries ago to the daintily embroidered scarves and cloths the early settlers took to the "meeting house" to put on the tables, altars, and lecterns. The same rule that applied for the nuns applied to the early settlers: Those who did the finest work were chosen to do the church linens.

As recently as fifty years ago, the ladies in many rural areas made exquisite linens that were taken to church each Sunday, used, and then returned home to be laundered for the following Sunday's use. In communities where there were several skilled needleworkers, the ladies took turns making and caring for the Sunday church linens. Today, especially in the Episcopal church, there are skilled embroiderers who still prefer to hand-embroider the fine linens for the altar. In some churches they are making needlepoint kneelers. Chances are

Monogrammed napkins often were made in sets of a dozen.

slim that the average person will ever see any of the fine old embroidery done by the convent nuns outside a museum. Actually there is not too much demand for the early linens as most have a religious motif, but they are excellent

Sideboard cloth done in colorful cross-stitch, circa 1940.

Pillow sham done in outline stitch.

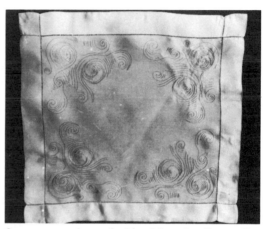

Square centerpiece embroidered in pale yellow outline stitch.

sources for studying what can be accomplished with only a needle, thread, and patience.

Kreuzstich stickerei is just another name for cross-stitch that was done on a heavy fabric using a specific pattern. It was more popular in Europe than in America, but some of the work was done here. Like all cross-stitch, the design could be made larger or smaller by covering more or fewer threads with the crosses.

Around 1905 a new type of embroidery was introduced under the name of *Copenhagen porcelain* embroidery. It was described as being a new and unique type of embroidery "that is being used with much interest in Copenhagen, the capital city of Denmark." Although there was little or no difference in the embroidery, apparently the white on white had become boring and shading was too tedious for the unskilled, so they were ready for the so-called "new" type of embroidery. Most of its appeal lay in the fact it was both simple and fast. Only four stitches were used: outline, buttonhole,

French knot, and satin stitch. They were done in three shades of blue on white fabric. Provided one used the correct shades of blue, the linens would perfectly match the Copenhagen china that was so popular at the time. This was the incentive the ladies needed, and they busied themselves with the production of everything from banquet-sized tablecloths to cheese and biscuit cozies in the new type of embroidery.

There are so many different kinds and varieties of *cutwork* embroidery, with one overlapping the other, that it could be confusing to the average collector. It is helpful to remember that very little of the centuries old cutwork is still available. Cutwork was originally called lace due to its airy appearance, and at one time

Some towels were monogrammed and the borders done in buttonhole stitch.

Close-up of French knot embroidery.

Small linen towel with cutwork design.

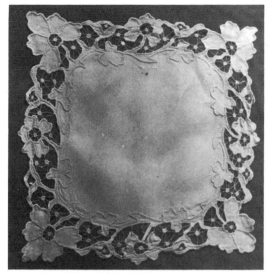

Finely done, early cutwork centerpiece, circa 1890.

Cutwork doily with border done in buttonhole stitch, then cut around rather than hemmed.

it was known as Richelieu work. In fact, it was from this work that pillow or needle lace originated. The first, of course, was made in the convents where the nuns carefully guarded the methods. At that time it was so fine and covered the fabric so completely that it did look like lace. Then around the fifteenth century,

End of ornately done cutwork dresser scarf.

Cutwork pillowcase with orchid design.

information on how to do cutwork became known to a few outsiders. Like any secret, once it leaked, it spread like wildfire. Now everybody began doing their version of cutwork. Turn-of-the-century cutwork was done by buttonhole stitching a design that was approximately one-eighth to as much as one-half of an inch wide, then cutting out the designated spaces. This created a light, airy, lacy piece of needlework that was enhanced by using it over a dark-colored fabric. It was found that old buttonhole scissors had yet another use: They were perfect for cutting the cutwork.

Fish scale was another type of embroidery that never gained too much popularity due to the great amount of work required in the actual preparation of the fish scales. Like the quills and feathers used in embroidery, the fish scales were genuine, and were taken from carp, perch, or any fish with brightly colored scales. If they weren't as bright and colorful as the ladies felt they should be, they simply dyed them as they had the quills. After the preliminary work was completed, two small holes were pierced in the top of each scale with a large needle. They were then sewn in a slightly overlapping fashion to effect the petals of a large flower, butterfly wings, or the wings of birds. There were two drawbacks that affected the popularity of this type embroidery: It only worked well on large designs, and there was

One of a three-piece cutwork vanity set.

danger of the scales falling off during laundering.

One type of embroidery that neither grew old nor lost its popularity was *French and eyelet.* A decade after the turn of the century one

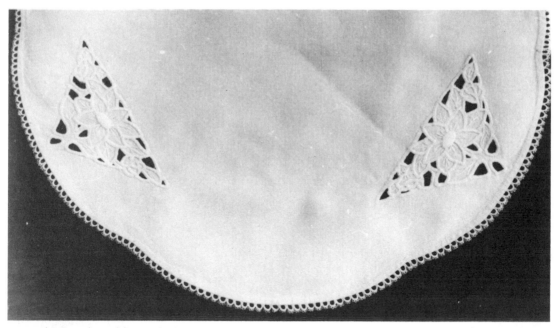

Cutwork centerpiece with tatted edging.

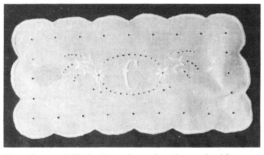

Bread tray doily in French and eyelet embroidery.

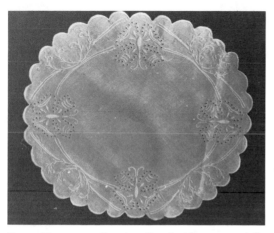

Butterflies were a favorite of embroiderers, especially when done in French and eyelet embroidery.

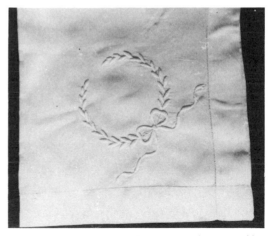

Corner of centerpiece made for Mission oak center tables.

authority said, "Every housewife wants at least one elaborately embroidered set of table linens in her linen chest to use on special occasions, and the careful needleworker can fulfill her heart's desire with comparatively little expense, for the prettiest, most durable and most satisfactory embroidered linens are those ornamented with French and eyelet embroidery." Perhaps the key word in that statement was "careful," as the prerequisites for this type of

Centerpiece with grape design done in French and eyelet embroidery.

embroidery were patience and meticulous workmanship. It was essential that one first learn to make perfect eyelets and then learn to do perfect satin stitch as the design is composed entirely of those two stitches. All the work had to be well padded, including the stems, if they were to be done in satin stitch (or solid stitch as it sometimes was called). Some preferred to do the stems in outline stitch, and pieces will be found with this third stitch, but generally it was done in just the two. Once the eyelets were "punched," they were completed in buttonhole stitch using a fine needle and thread. It was generally done in white on white.

Japanese embroidery was quite similar to the Chinese work—which makes sense since they were the only two peoples with enough patience to do the intricate and exquisite work. Their work is even more commendable when

one realizes they often did the intricate designs without a stamped figure or even an outline. What is even more amazing is the fact that these patternless designs were embroidered on figured fabric. To be able to embroider a small, intricate design on a small piece of figured fabric requires more talent and skill than the average person will ever know. Most of their work was done on silk fabric with silk or gold thread. Much of the gold cord was couched on to fill in the backgrounds. Again, there was a great deal of difference in the work they made for their own use and that exported to the Western world. Since the stork was considered a sacred bird, it frequently was used in their work, making it a little easier to separate Japanese embroidery from the Chinese. The bird usually was worked in white silk shading to gray or black.

Japanese embroidery is filled with flow-

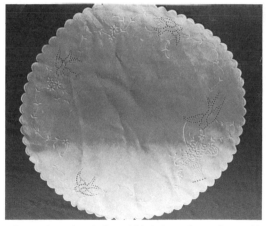

Flowers in satin stitch and birds in eyelet make up this centerpiece.

French and eyelet embroidered centerpiece with different butterfly design.

Both doilies have the same design, but eyelets in one make a noticeable difference.

One end of an exquisite scarf with heavy satin-stitch embroidery surrounding the drawn work.

ers, with the cherry and hawthorn the most popular. They also used human figures extensively in the work they kept at home, and some appeared on export work. They were adept at getting every feature correct, down to the last

Counted cross-stitch embroidery was used on this piece.

Mountmellick centerpiece.

wrinkle on the face. This was accomplished by using raised lines of a slightly different color than the flesh-colored silk used on the balance of the face. The best of the Chinese and Japanese embroideries found here now were the ones brought back years ago by visitors and missionaries to the two countries.

Around 1880 the nuns in a convent in Mountmellick in Ireland created a new type of embroidery. It was quite elaborate with many

Close-up of the design.

Modified Mountmellick embroidery.

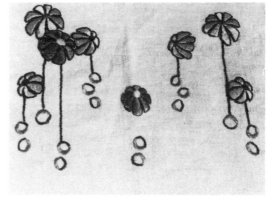

Satin-stitched pillow top, circa 1910.

fancy stitches like cable plait, double bullion, wheat ear, cable and herringbone, thorn, and cable plait with overcasting. As was the custom in those days, the children and the poor women of the parish went to the convent to learn and to embroider fine linens. Soon this group was so proficient that they decided to form an industrial association to sell their work.

In 1885, when the Princess of Wales went to Ireland for a visit, she was given a piece of this embroidery. By then it had become known as *Mountmellick* embroidery. The princess was so impressed with the work, she took it home to show her friend. This was the launching it needed. Soon all of England and America was engrossed in making this new type of embroidery, and those who found it too difficult

On colored floral embroidery, shading was of the utmost importance.

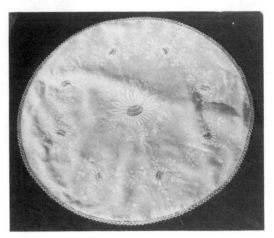

Heavily embroidered centerpiece.

Small triangular piece with heavy embroidery, factory-made lace on one side, and Irish crochet on the other. Use unknown.

bought pieces made by the ladies in the convent. It was so specialized that it required special thread.

Corticelli made the threads and named them Mountmellick embroidery silks. The letter F denoted the finest, FF and G were the medium weights, and H was the coarsest. Most of the work was done in white on white, but a little was done in the special blue thread. Since the work was quite heavy, it was suggested that it be done on a heavier fabric, with white satin jean fabric recommended as the best. It might have been a heavy type of embroidery, but it was recommended for use on everything from night dress sachets to pinafores. It was suggested that smaller designs and finer thread be used on most clothing with linen, sateen, and cashmere. Bold florals were used, with the favorites being passionflower, sunflower, and lilies. The flowers were usually worked in high raised satin stitch and were embellished with French knots and other fancy stitches. The leaves would be done partially in satin stitch with the veins done in cat, brier, or coral stitch.

Tent stitch or old canvas embroidery was used to make this motto that was framed around 1860.

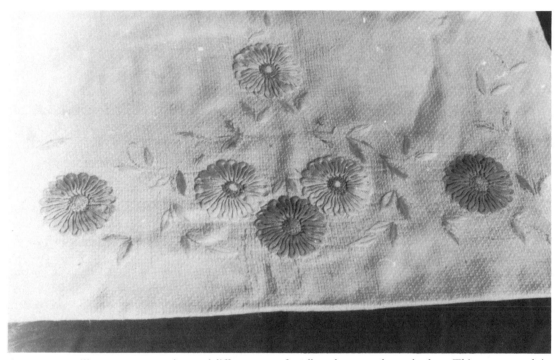

A century ago pillows were very popular, and different types of needlework were used to make them. This one was made in Rococo or China ribbon embroidery.

Perforated cardboard embroidery was one of the simplest types of embroidery and had fewer uses than most other types. The cardboard was purchased, cut to the desired size (usually a bookmarker), and then worked. The motto, sentimental quote, or the person's name was done in tent stitch or cross-stitch. Silk thread was the preferred type, but light wool often was used. For the fancier pieces a floral border could be added. It could be left plain or the back could be covered with ribbon or silk fabric.

Rococo embroidery, also known as *China ribbon* embroidery, was another specialty type. It was done by embroidering the design with the so-called China ribbon, a very narrow ribbon measuring about one-eighth of an inch in width. It was threaded through a large needle and actually worked through the fabric after holes had been made with a stilleto. The

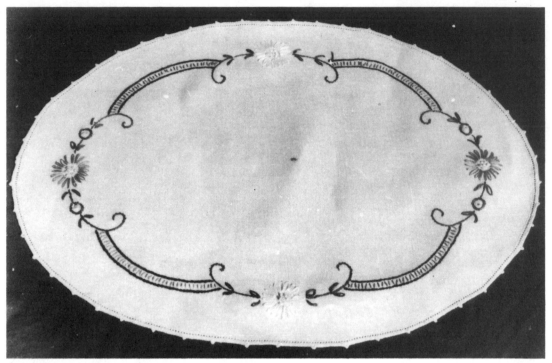

Young people are especially fond of this type of embroidery because they can remember their grandmothers making it in the 1950s and 1960s.

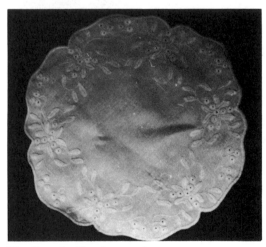

Heavily embroidered centerpiece.

ribbon was laid flat to form the flowers and leaves while the stems were embroidered in outline stitch. French knots, made with thread, were used in the centers of the flowers. This was such a fancy embroidery that it was only used on special types of clothing that were made of silks, satins, and velvets. Apparently one of the reasons it never became too popular was the cost—as the ribbon was much more expensive than thread.

Just as there were special threads for the Mountmellick embroidery, there were other special threads made for specific types of embroidery. The choice of threads depended on the needs and sometimes the whims of the maker as well as the fabric that was being used. Although special thread was recommended for the Mountmellick embroidery, it was possible for an advanced embroiderer to change the design somewhat and still embroider it with regular thread. Most rules and suggestions were given for the beginners and those not advanced enough to be able to make the necessary changes to convert a design from one fabric to another or from one type of thread to another.

Among the many types of thread available a century ago, silks were the most popular. Silk embroidery thread could be bought in amounts that ranged from a small spool to hanks averaging 840 yards each. It was made in a variety of colors and types.

The most common and widely used type was the simple embroidery silk that came in "five hundred different shades and grades" according to one thread company's ad. They offered a sample book listing all the shades and grades for a mere 5¢. Embroiderers were advised to order from the book, not send the "goods to be matched to the thread."

Rope silk was described as "the heaviest thread employed in embroidery." It was a heavy, rather loose twisted silk that was used on heavy fabric and large designs. Price for rope silk in 1890 was 50¢ for one dozen skeins.

The etching or outline silk was only about half the size of regular silk embroidery thread. It had a harder twist than regular thread and featured more gloss and less fuzz. The price was 40¢ for one dozen skeins.

English twisted heavy embroidery thread was a coarse, heavy thread that was highly recommended for work on plush, woolens, and velvets. As all embroiderers know, most thread can be split to do finer work, and this was one of the easiest to split. All the silks were advertised as fast colors (they were not supposed to fade in either soap and water or sunlight). This silk sold for 40¢ per dozen skeins.

Filo silk floss, sometimes called floss silk, was a six-strand slack twisted silk that was extremely smooth and glossy. It was made from the choice threads unwound from the cocoons, making it the best of the silk thread—which was reflected in the price of 60¢ for a dozen skeins in 1890.

One firm offered hanks (840 yards) of silk embroidery thread for the small sum of 50¢ each. This was a considerable savings for the embroiderer who used large amounts in one color.

Filoselle, also called spun silk, was one of the cheapest of the silk embroidery threads as it was made from the outside coverings of the cocoons mixed with other discarded silks. It was carded and spun like cotton and wool and was sold for much less than the better grades of silk. It is believed the cheaper price could have influenced its popularity, as sales of filoselle

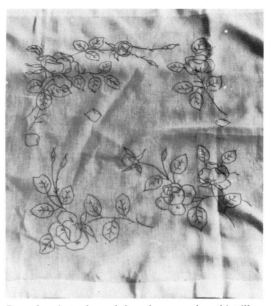

Roses done in turkey red thread were used on this pillow sham.

more than doubled those of silk floss during the decades before and after the turn of the century.

Another silk thread, called purse silk or silk twist, could be used either for ordinary sewing or for embroidery, but it was used mostly for crocheting purses. It was a thick, twisted thread that included instructions on the wrapper for several types of embroidery, but there was a notation that it worked better on certain stitches.

Embroidery cotton was made in sizes that ranged from No. 4 to No. 100, and was made in as many shades as the silk. Most merchants did not, however, guarantee colors and shades like olives, yellows, pinks, and greens to be "wash colors" or fast colors. The truth was they might or might not fade when washed and hung in direct sunlight. The price in 1890 was 25¢ for thirty skeins.

In 1890 it was noted that "short length, slack twisted, poor grade half-cotton silks sell for what they will bring," and one company offered them for the reasonable price of 85¢ for one hundred skeins.

Crewel embroidery thread originally was a loosely twisted worsted type of yarn. It was used as early as the seventeenth century for

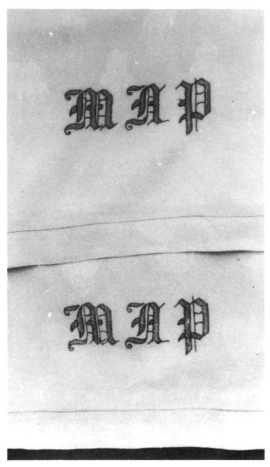

Pair of large towels done in turkey red embroidery.

Portion of hand-loomed bedspread woven of wool thread and embroidered in wool thread with crocheted wool border, circa 1875.

embroidering bed hangings, curtains, and furniture covers. Around 1900 it came in three sizes. The first, called a tapestry crewel, was soft and smooth. Medium crewel was an appropriate name for the second size, which came in approximately 300 different shades. A fine crewel was used for the smaller designs. All of these were sold by the hank, which in this case was 560 yards. The amount in a hank of thread varied according to the weight.

There were several types of flax or linen thread, but none were used extensively in embroidery. It was suggested by the very early embroiderers that if the homespun linen

One piece of sideboard set embroidered in chain stitch with crocheted border.

thread was boiled for a short period of time it would soften enough to work well. Apparently the stiffness was one of the features that detracted from its use. One type of commercially made thread was called flax thread. It was described as a silky thread, indicating that some type of silk was mixed with the flax. Embroiderers were said to like it.

These are by no means all the types of embroidery made during the Victorian era, nor is the list of threads complete, but these were the most popular in both categories.

CHAPTER 8
Battenberg, the Royal Lace

It might not sound as fancy as some of the names given other laces, but Battenberg also can be called "speed lace" because it could be made quickly when compared to the months and years required to make pillow lace.

The term "lace" was included in the name of many types of light, airy needlework, especially that used for borders and edgings. Workers usually referred to it by the type of work—like crocheted lace, hairpin lace, tatted lace, knitted lace, or pillow lace. Then there were the so-called laces made with braids and fancy stitchery. First and foremost among these was the one called Battenberg. It was and still is so well known that most braid work is lumped under that name.

Battenberg, also known as Royal Battenberg and Renaissance lace, was a late bloomer in the needlework field and was created circa the last decade of the nineteenth century. It is the one type of needlework that can be described as all-American as it was the brainchild of New Yorker Sara Hadley, who conceived and created the first Battenberg lace.

There has been some question as to the exact date it was first made and the exact origin of the name. Some say it was called Royal Battenberg because it was created at the time of the wedding of Princess Beatrice, youngest daughter of Queen Victoria, to Prince Henry of Battenberg. There are others who claim it received its name from the widowed Princess Beatrice, who found much consolation in doing this work after the early death of her husband. Regardless of how they settled on the name, it is so beautiful that it deserves the royal title.

Imitation is the sincerest form of flattery, they say, but Battenberg, though extremely popular, was not copied as much as it was varied. Different types of braid soon were introduced along with a variety of stitches. New names like Modern Point, Honiton, Duchesse, Cluny, Brabant, and others developed as well. Each was almost identical to Battenberg but was named for the type of braid used to make it.

Unless one is preparing to collect only braid laces, it is really not necessary to learn all the different types of braids and stitches, but it does help to have a working knowledge of them.

It was not until around 1906 that any name other than Battenberg was used for a braid lace. Writers and needleworkers called all pieces either Battenberg or Royal Battenberg. One writer in 1898 described it as one segment of needlework that "will ever be classed among those refined arts peculiarly adapted to the deftness and delicacy of woman's handiwork." Statements like that are one of the reasons all types of needlework are now called "Womantiques" and so avidly sought by women. Needlework is the one antique item they can claim as their own; one that was made by their own. The 1898 writer continued, "In the choice and care of her Battenberg stands revealed the index of a woman's innate refinement and good taste."

In 1900 one writer commented, "The rage for lace making which began with Royal Battenberg appears to have grown most rapidly and continues unabated. It is a pastime resulting in something practical as well as beautiful, something valuable enough to become an heirloom, if skillfully made from the best materials and by a first-class design." The writer had no idea what a wise statement she was making, nor in her wildest imagination could she have visualized how collectors today would search for and treasure the Battenberg being made then.

The original Battenberg was made with one basic foundation stitch: buttonhole picot. The method for working these Battenberg bars was simple and a bit slow, but not nearly as slow as the other laces. For each space that had to be filled with bars, the worker started at any convenient point in the braid after it had been basted to the pattern. The thread was carried to another point along the edge, forming a sort of semitaut loop about one-third to one-half inch long. There it was fastened to the other side. The thread was then carried to the first point and back again so there would be three threads in each bar. Next, a buttonhole (embroidery) stitch was made over the bar at the center. Then a picot was made by wrapping the thread around the needle twelve times (similar to the French knot) and pulling the picot tight. It then was fastened with another buttonhole stitch. The needleworker could make another bar from this last buttonhole stitch using the same method she used to make the first bar. After this bar was made, the buttonhole stitch and picot were repeated. This continued around the braid until most of the space was filled. When the last bar was completed, the worker returned to the unfinished half of the first one, where she completed it along with any other incomplete ones.

Although most needleworkers use a pattern in any type of needlework, experienced workers always have been able to make the decision and then follow it up with appropriate stitches, provided they felt more or less were needed. Usually it is very easy to add a few more stitches when it is believed they will add to the attractiveness of the work. In the case of Battenberg, adding more bars was a very easy chore.

Another popular stitch or design used in Battenberg and other braid laces was the flat wheel, spider, or flat rosette. All three names were used in instructions, but the directions

for making them were the same. They were made or formed on the thread that had been twisted twice across the space between the braids. As many threads as were necessary could be used, then caught at the center with a single thread that was woven in and out or over and under until the wheel or spider reached the desired size.

If one preferred rings (or "buttons" as they were often called) rather than the spiders or rosettes, they could be made by wrapping linen thread around a pencil five times, then working over it closely with a buttonhole embroidery stitch.

All the braid laces were made to imitate the real thing. French Irish was no exception. It was a newer lace, and a new stitch called Irish background was created along with it. It was a rather complicated stitch, but this braid lace often was used to make hats. Since the ladies seldom left home without a hat in those days, they thought it was well worth the extra effort. Who could miss milady's fancy stitchery when it was being worn on her head?

Other stitches—some different, others identical—were given different names by the people who created or used them. As with all types of needlework, there were those workers who did excellent work, with their stitches made perfectly and according to instructions. Then there were those who could not or would not learn, and others who simply didn't have the ability to do quality work. More poor quality pieces will be found in other types of needlework than in Battenberg, as most of these pieces show expert workmanship.

Some preparatory work had to be done before the actual stitchery began. First, the worker had to decide if she had the ability to create her own design. If not, she had to purchase one already stamped. Materials had to be bought, and workers were cautioned to buy only the very best types of braid. Pieces could be made in all silk, all linen, or even a mixture of the two because in those early days cotton was not used. Reportedly cotton was difficult to work with and would not hold its shape. Silk or linen braids worked with silk or linen threads were considered the best. They would look prettier and last longer.

Although braid laces were easier and

Pink muslin pattern with Battenberg in progress.

One end of an elaborately done Battenberg piano scarf.

quicker to make than the old pillow laces, the intricate designs still required many weeks of patient labor. When all the materials had been acquired, there was still the time-consuming task of basting the braid on the design. Shortly after the turn of the century, one could buy any of a number of patterns stamped on pink or white muslin. The design, where the braids were to be basted, was stamped along with designs for the various stitches that should be used. Braids that previously had been in limited supply now could be bought in any width. The correct width and color were basted securely onto the pattern before the fancy stitchery was begun.

The term "basting" is a misnomer when discussing braid laces because it was much better to use a close running stitch when securing the braid to the pattern. The stitches had to be close and they had to be small to hold the braid in shape or the design would not be correct. An occasional backstitch was recommended to keep the braid securely in place. Extra stitches were required on the outer edges of curves, as they had a tendency to become loose as the work progressed. Nearly all the fancy braids had drawing threads or strings on the edges, which made it easy to shape the

braid into flower petals, leaves, circles, and curliques.

One rule stated in many magazine articles on Battenberg—sew the pattern onto leather or some strong fabric before basting on the braid—was ignored by advanced needleworkers. They ignored it because they had found something that worked better and cost less: heavy brown wrapping paper.

Perhaps the one thing most needleworkers found unusual with making Battenberg and all braid laces was the fact that all work had to be done "wrong side out." The side of the braid showing on the pattern would, when finished, be the underside. The worker had to reverse her regular working procedure to enable her to make the perfect stitches on the bottom, not on the top as she would in all other types of needlework.

In those days materials needed to make braid laces could be more expensive than materials for other types of needlework. Cost estimates to make various pieces show the material for a piano scarf with the fabric bordered with

Elaborate Battenberg bertha or collar.

Battenberg would cost around $10. It would cost approximately $2.50 a yard to make hat lace, while the materials needed to made an ordinary collar would cost $3.

Not all the fancy stitchery was done in silk and linen threads. Some of the fancier pieces, like theater bags, often had an intermingling of gold thread for that touch of luxury and elegance. That naturally increased the price of the bag.

Oftentimes a glimpse into old instruction books will give collectors insights into the problems and work involved in making some of the many needlework pieces we now collect. A simple look at the directions for making a braid lace theater bag shows how gathering the materials could become involved and expensive. It was suggested that the bag be lined with "fine white brocaded satin with a flower in delicate shades scattered here and there." But if the maker was unable to find this brocaded satin or could not afford it since it was very expensive, then she was to buy all-white brocaded satin and "tint it with water colors using any dainty color combination." Along with the satin she had to buy two-and-one-half yards of

pink satin ribbon for the drawstrings and eight ivory rings to be attached to the bag to hold the ribbon drawstrings. Now she had to make the Battenberg lace to be used on either side of the bag.

Even though braid laces were originally used on household linens, they were later used on many types of clothing. In fact, many items were made entirely of the laces. One of the most popular was hats, and next were the collars, cuffs, berthas, and chemisettes (a sort of vest similar to the dickies of the 1940s). Fine braid lace was a favorite for baby caps and yokes for summer dresses. This was a time when "A thing worth doing at all was worth doing well," and with that thought in mind the expert needleworker created and made the correct article of clothing to wear for each and every occasion. Proof of that is the chafing apron made to wear when using the chafing dish. Both tea and chafing aprons had borders of Battenberg lace, while others only had appliqués of the lace tacked on. Corset covers and underbodices as well as petticoats were favorites for the lace makers.

One example of braid work at its showiest

was when it was done on net, and one of the most beautiful pieces we've seen was made by an early worker who edged a net scarf with braid lace and tacked braid lace appliqués all over the scarf. The most becoming way to wear it, the owner said, was to place the center at the front of the neck, cross it on the back, bring both ends to the front, and tie it once or simply fasten it with a brooch.

Pieces of braid work most often found today will be round tablecloths. Everybody had at least one round table where the cloth could be shown to advantage. No old towels have been seen with this decoration, but that doesn't rule out the possibility they were made. If Battenberg was used on pillowcases or pillow shams, none have been found. Actually, shams were being phased out by the time Battenberg became popular, but doilies and centerpieces were favorites, as were dresser scarves.

Some ladies made Battenberg doilies and centerpieces for use in the ever-popular china cabinets. There they served a dual role: They not only enhanced the beauty of the glass and china in the cabinets, but they also provided the perfect spot to show off one's handiwork without seeming to boast.

There also were accomplished needle-workers who simply could not afford the expensive materials required to make genuine Battenberg. They devised what they called a "simulated" Battenberg lace that was actually a combination of embroidery stitches. Some pieces were so well done it was hard to tell them from the real thing at a distance. The simulated braid was done entirely in plain buttonhole stitch, while the lacy portion was created with a combination of honeycomb, brier, spider, and a few fancy cross-stitches. The work usually was done on fine linen, and in some cases the worker embroidered flowers on top of the simulated lace. The floral embroidery always was done in silk threads of various shades.

There were differences of opinion among many of the early Battenberg makers as to the correct procedure for ironing the work the first time. Some felt it would hold its shape better if

Large, round Battenberg tablecloth. Buttons or rings were used to make the grape design.

Battenberg tablecloth with different design.

Battenberg centerpiece.

Square Battenberg centerpiece.

Battenberg doily.

it was ironed *before* it was removed from the pattern and the wrapping paper. Others insisted it was better to remove it from the pattern and paper before the ironing began. Those who removed their work before ironing had a special method. Once the paper and pattern had been removed, the lace was placed right side down on several thicknesses of soft muslin. A cloth soaked in hot borax water and then wrung out was placed on top, and it was ironed with a hot iron. This supposedly gave it the same fresh look found on ready-made laces.

There might have been some controversy over the correct ironing procedures, but there never was any question as to the correct process for laundering the laces. Great care must be taken, they said, in the cleaning of Battenberg and other braid laces. It never should be rubbed with the hands or scrubbed in any fashion. Instead, it should be soaked in cold water in an earthen bowl or pot and allowed to simmer only (*never* boil) on the back of the woodburning stove until the soiled parts appeared clean. All soap—and nothing other than pure soap was used—had to be removed from the lace. The pot with fresh water and the Battenberg was returned to the back of the stove, where it simmered for another hour. It was then rinsed in fresh water a few times and hung out to dry partially. While it was still damp, it was ironed, always on the wrong side, with a hot iron. Before the ironing

began the lace had to be stretched carefully by hand and all picots drawn into place. Then and only then was the soft white muslin cloth placed over the lace and the ironing begun.

Antique collectors won't be able to find tools connected with this work, as Battenberg was made with only a needle and thread. A thimble was used when necessary but was not essential. Any kind of scissors were used to cut threads. No hoops or frames were used as the pattern was basted on heavy wrapping paper. There is a good, if not ample, supply of old Battenberg available if one is willing to search. Most needlework is still reasonably priced considering it is one of the last handmade antiques left, but prices have risen sharply during the past year.

During the past several years new Battenberg has been coming in from China. These new pieces have been seen in department stores with the "Made in China" labels intact and among old linens in antiques shows, malls, and shops with the labels removed. Yet it is very easy to distinguish the new from the old. The new is much stiffer than the old, even after washing. The work is good but not nearly as good as our antique Battenberg. New Chinese-made pieces most often seen are towels, which are scarce to nonexistent in old Battenberg, as well as pillow tops, collars, cuffs, doilies, and centerpieces.

CHAPTER 9
The Variety of Drawn Work

During the twelfth century it was called *opus tiratum,* but by the nineteenth century Victorian ladies had simplified the name to drawn work, a very descriptive name. It is almost impossible to mistake this work or not be able to recognize it on sight because it is exactly what the name implies: threads drawn from the fabric and fancy designs created on the remaining ones.

Drawn work is one of the older types of needlework. The exact date it was created or introduced has been lost in the mist of antiquity. It is probably about as old as embroidery, because women began trying to find different methods of decorating fabric as soon as they learned how to spin and weave wool, flax, and cotton. Drawn work was an easy method because no extra materials were required other than working thread which could, in many cases, be the thread drawn from the fabric in the first place. It is known to have been done as early as the twelfth century, maybe earlier, and has continued to be a favorite among needleworkers since.

Like all types of needlework it has had its ups and downs in popularity, often because a new type of needlework became a craze. Another reason why its popularity might decline could be the amount of tedious work and concentrated effort required to make it. But drawn work is as much a staple to needlework as cornbread is to a southerner.

Drawn work, like embroidery, was done over a long period of time by people all over the world. It is still being made, but in very limited quantities.

The names by which it was known are as varied as the people who made it. One of the names, Hamburg point, would indicate it was made by German workers. Another, Broderie de Nancy, was the name given drawn work in France, or it might have been the name used by the Flemish workers who were so skilled in all types of needlework and became famous because of the school they founded to train needleworkers. At one time the work was called "Dresden point," no doubt for the town of Dresden where so much beautiful china was made. Dresden china presented on Dresden point tablecloths would have been a breathtaking sight. Other names by which drawn work was known through the years include Indian work (thought to have originated in India), Tonder point, and Ponto Tirato, another of the very early names.

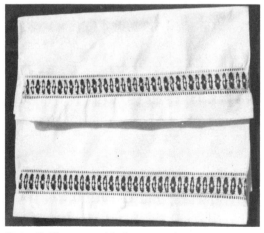

Pair of pillowcases with drawn work.

Piano scarves were popular among drawn work makers, perhaps because they were one of the most visible pieces in the house.

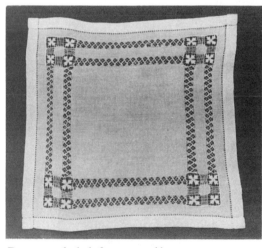

Drawn work cloth for a tea table.

Close-up of one corner of the cloth.

The early work was so fine and so beautiful that it looked more like lace than some of the later, poorly made lace. The work was done on fine linen with almost half the threads being drawn so the needleworker could made a hon-

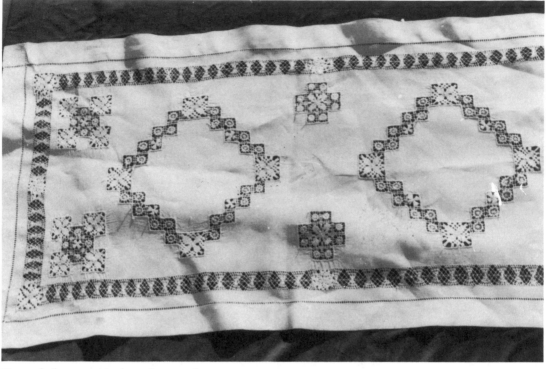

One end of an ornately done piano scarf.

eycomb design on which to work the exquisite floral patterns. During the early years drawn work was combined with embroidery to make some of the richest church linens and vestments known. In later years it still was exquisite, but the work had become larger and the designs less intricate. These larger designs probably were intricate enough for the average housewife, who could spend only so many hours a day on her needlework—hours sandwiched between getting meals, doing laundry, and other household chores. She was not like the nuns and workers in the early convent days, who spent every hour of every day busily working on their needlework.

One of the most interesting things about drawn work is the fact that a person can take a piece of fabric and make an outstanding piece of needlework with nothing but a needle and some thread. Poor-quality fabric never was recommended for drawn work because too much work was involved to take chances with it.

The fabric was about the only expense involved in making drawn work. The thread, at 10¢ for a 200-yard spool, was so inexpensive that it was hardly worth counting. A yard of fine linen could be bought in those days for less than 50¢, so for around $1.00 one could buy enough fabric to make a set of luncheon doilies for six place settings. The set would include the doilies for the service plate, bread and butter plates, and one for each tumbler.

Drawn work doilies and centerpieces were made in large numbers, as they were in embroidery. However, they apparently were not made in as large numbers if one is to judge by the examples available today. The amount of work required to make drawn work pieces might have been a determining factor. It was slow, tedious, and time consuming as half the threads in the design had to be drawn out while the remainder were fastened together with designs worked in them. In terms of materials costs, this was one of the least expensive types of needlework, but it required as much if not more tedious work than the others.

Embroidery designs could be big and

Small centerpiece with two rows of double hemstitching around the edge.

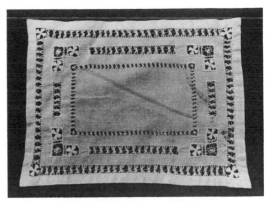

Small oblong centerpiece.

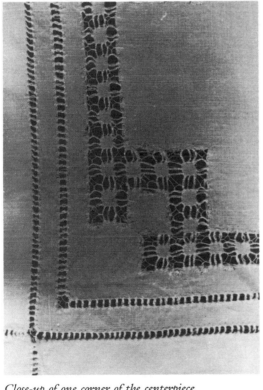

Close-up of one corner of the centerpiece.

bold, and the braids used to make Battenberg filled part of the design. In drawn work, however, nothing filled the design but tiny stitches, each made by hand one at a time. The thread used to make drawn work was much finer and required more stitches to accomplish the same effect than any other type of needlework.

Drawn work pieces are always square or rectangular since it is impossible to pull the threads in any other direction. Either the woof or the warf threads can be pulled. On many pieces, especially the small ones, the threads were drawn a short distance from the edge so the hem could be turned up and caught with the hemstitching. On these pieces there is always a narrow row of hemstitching around the edge, with the bottom stitching catching the edge of the hem. On some pieces there will be two narrow rows of hemstitching around the edge about one-quarter of an inch apart. Some have plain centers, others embroidered centers, while the majority have elaborate drawn work designs in the center.

Drawn work lessons always began with the hemstitched border. In fact, in an effort to perfect that stitch, many young girls a century ago filled their dower or hope chests with dozens of napkins with hemstitched borders. If they were well trained in satin stitch, they also monogrammed one corner.

Since hemstitching was more or less the basic or background stitch for drawn work, it was absolutely essential that the beginner master it first. To fully appreciate the old drawn work pieces found today, it is necessary for the collector to understand how much practice and patience went into the work. Maybe the directions for making a row of hemstitching will best illustrate the amount of work required

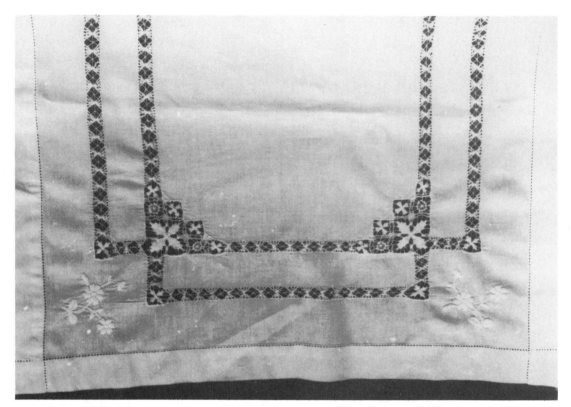

End of piano scarf showing both the drawn work and the embroidery.

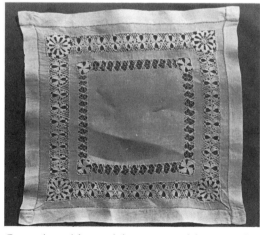

Centerpiece with two elaborate rows of drawn work.

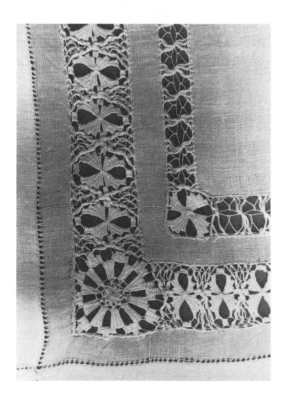

Close-up of one corner of the centerpiece.

The design on this centerpiece is a four-leaf clover.

stitch, which is made by fastening the working thread in the fabric, was continued by bringing it around toward the left like a circle and passing the needle under the threads of the fabric and under the working thread. When this was pulled tight it formed a knot stitch. This held the drawn threads in place and also almost made each stitch an individual one. Hemstitching is the basic stitch in drawn work, yet the knot stitch is the ingredient that makes the hemstitch possible. The worker continued to make these stitches all around the border.

If only one side of the work was completed, it was called single hemstitching. Most pieces will have both sides of the drawn section completed, but there are exceptions. Quite often a second row of hemstitching was added, especially on the larger pieces.

Small pieces, like tumbler doilies and napkins (the smaller napkins, not the large twenty-four-inch square napkins), with only one row of hemstitching could be done by an experienced needleworker without any aids other than a needle, thread, and maybe a thimble, if she was accustomed to using one. When the worker felt some type of holder for the smaller pieces was necessary, she could use embroidery hoops. When making the larger pieces, however, both the experienced and the inexperienced worker needed a frame.

The frames for drawn work were quite similar to those used for embroidery. About the only difference between them, if both types were purchased either from the "fancy goods store" or the mail order department of the various needlework magazines, was the fact that the wooden frames for drawn work would be wrapped in soft fabric.

Today, some of the advice for obtaining frames, especially the prices quoted nearly a century ago, can evoke a smile. For instance, one writer giving instructions for making drawn work in 1890 stated, "If the frames for drawn work are not obtainable in your area, almost any hardware merchant or plumber will make, for about fifteen cents, a frame of boiler wire, bent in shape with ends welded together." Once this frame or any other made-to-order frame was taken home, the worker had to wrap it with strips of soft cotton cloth torn

to make one small border on a napkin. First, a piece of fabric was cut to the desired size. Once the piece had been squared (cut on a straight line along one thread), six threads were pulled or drawn from each side, one-eighth of an inch from the edge on each of the four sides. After the fabric had been turned down about one-eighth of an inch, a one-half-inch hem was basted into place. Beginning on the left side of the napkin, the worker fastened the thread, taking care to ensure that the knot in the working thread was well hidden. In drawn work all knots and backstitching had to be hidden or they would detract from the design.

The labor-saving part of this work was the fact that the hem could be fastened into place with the stitches that were a part of the hemstitching. After the worker had hidden the knot, the needle was placed under five or six threads (depending on the fabric and design). Working from right to left, the needle was drawn through to make an ordinary hemming stitch and then tied with a knot stitch. The knot straight, not on the bias. Husbands also built soft wood frames for their wives. In cases where the husband built the frames, he might build several in assorted sizes. Among the advertised frames, the size most commonly recommended was eighteen inches long and eight inches wide.

All makers of drawn work were especially conscious of the differences in the quality of linen threads. Unless flax had been spun carefully, it would not be smooth. This could happen with machine-made thread as well as that spun at home. Since drawn work required such fine stitches, it was essential for the worker to have smooth, even-textured thread.

Like all other types of needlework, drawn work also was known for its fancy-named patterns and designs. One intricate block design often was called Japanese work. Before beginning on this design, the worker took small squares of cardboard and marked off with a pencil the blocks to be drawn and worked. Opposite ends of the block were cut with fine scissors and the short threads were pulled from one direction, leaving those running in the opposite direction for the design. Another type of block work had blocks so small that cardboard could not be used. In this case one counted the threads, usually cutting and drawing five and leaving five on which to work the design. Even in these small spaces, advanced workers made intricate designs.

It seems that the majority of workers creating drawn work around the turn of the century preferred the larger designs because they were faster and easier to make. It still took weeks to complete one piece, but this was considerably faster than the early, intricate designs that required many months of work.

The small block design often was referred to as an "antique design," a reference to an earlier design probably used during the eighteenth century.

There was another revival of drawn work around 1825. At that time some of the most beautiful and most intricate work in this field was being done by nuns in Cuba. Rich brides almost refused to be married unless the lingerie in their trousseaus was trimmed with dainty drawn work from the Cuban convents. That

Centerpiece with block design called Japanese work.

fashion, like others before and after it, seems to have run its course and died out.

Drawn work was not mentioned in books on needlework in the mid-eighteenth century. But it became fashionable again around 1890. That revival was best described by one needleworker, who wrote in *Home Needlework Magazine* in 1895 that, "It has been many years since drawn work has been in vogue, until recently, and like a mushroom it has seemed to spring up as in a night's growth, and is now being adapted to so many decorative purposes. Each room of the house claims appropriately some design in this work, beginning downstairs and ending in my lady's chamber."

There were few stitches that could be called basic drawn work stitches. The most important, of course, was the hemstitch. Then there were the rosettes or spiders made similar to those used in making Battenberg. The most popular motifs for the corners were the Maltese cross and the star. If enough thread was not left in the corners after the drawn threads were removed, the worker could add more by carefully working them into the edge of the drawn fabric. Then with an over-and-under, weaving type of stitch she could make any design she chose. One worker described making the Maltese cross as being exactly like darning her cotton stockings—in and out, back and forth over the threads.

Experienced needleworkers always have

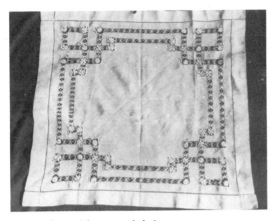

Centerpiece with unusual design.

Cloth for tea table.

experimented and created new stitches or variations of old ones. The same applied to drawn work. One lady even went so far as to make a sampler of the various stitches she had created. It made an interesting picture and could be used to refresh her memory on various stitches. Rather than make a design on the thread like a star, cross, or spider, some would make a design of the threads by pulling them into various shapes and running threads through the center. Or, they might work a sort of chain stitch through the center and pull several strands of thread into different designs. As with all types of needlework, the drawn work maker, if she was skilled, could create something novel and different for both her home and her wearing apparel.

In some of the large designs, the old buttonhole (embroidery) stitch was used. Complete squares were cut out of the fabric, buttonholed around, and then the correct number of threads added to make the desired motif. In rare incidents very small, plain buttonholed squares alternated with squares of the same size, with the latter having a design in the center.

Most of the antique drawn work pieces that were made around one hundred years ago and are found today will be done in white on white, although occasionally colored pieces will be found. On such pieces the background often was in color, like an ecru linen or muslin centerpiece with the stitchery done in yellow

Close-up of corner of tea-table cloth.

and orange, or a soft yellow piece with shades of green and brown.

Contrary to the rules established for making most white drawn work using linen thread on linen fabric and later cotton thread on

Tea-table cloth with another design.

Close-up of one corner.

cotton fabric, silk thread was used exclusively on the colored drawn work regardless of the content of the fabric. It seems that more squares were cut and buttonholed in the colored work than in the white. Perhaps those ingenious ladies had a reason for that: The colors showed up more prominently in buttonhole stitch than in hemstitch, thereby making the colored pieces very attractive. Again it must be emphasized that there were no rigid rules in needlework. Pieces usually were made to fit the needs and taste of the maker.

The majority of the drawn work pieces found today will be small tablecloths, doilies, and centerpieces. Handkerchiefs and pillows—the so-called "sofa pillows"—were also favorites of the drawn work makers. Drawn work was extremely popular as gifts. Towels and splashers have been found with every type of drawn work, from single hemstitching to elaborate designs two and three inches wide. Drawn work was used on nightgown yokes, around the tops of corset covers, and on the bottom of both petticoats and pantaloons. Blouses, or "waists" as grandmother called them, might have a series of diamond-shaped pieces down the front that had been intricately done in drawn work.

Like all needlework, drawn work was combined with other types of needlework. Drawn work centerpieces will be found with borders of crocheted, knitted, or tatted lace, and it was the rule rather than the exception to monogram towels with drawn work borders. Many will be found with embroidered monograms; drawn work borders just above the hem; and crocheted, tatted, or knitted lace on the edge.

Just as many of the various types of needlework are now experiencing a revival, it could happen to drawn work. All that is needed is for one person to get the idea to make some pieces for her home or some "heirlooms of tomorrow" and spread the word. One of the reasons fewer women are doing needlework today is the fact that so many are working outside the home, which leaves precious little time for intricate needlework.

However, if someone did decide to start making drawn work again, and wanted old instructions, our suggestion would be to search for old needlework books and magazines. They often can be found at antiques shows, shops, malls, and flea markets. Check the table of contents because not all of them

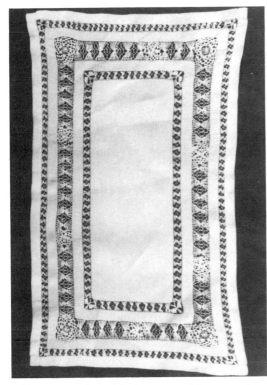

Oblong centerpiece with three rows of drawn work.

Close-up of towel with monogram and drawn work.

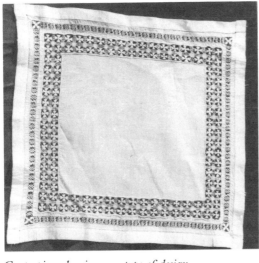

Centerpiece showing one type of design.

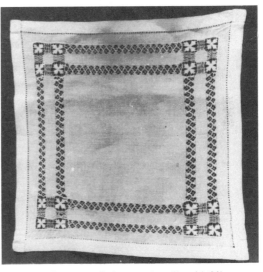

Intricate drawn work done on handkerchief linen.

have information on all types of work. In fact, drawn work was omitted from several. An example is Mrs. Pullan's *The Lady's Manual of Fancy Work,* published in 1858. It covers needlework and crafts from appliqué to potichiomanie, but there is not one about drawn work.

Apparently, drawn work experienced its greatest revival during the last quarter of the nineteenth century, or at least more written

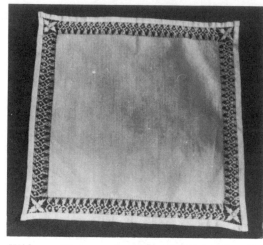

Wide row of drawn work on lawn (fabric) handkerchief.

Fringed doily with drawn work on handkerchief linen.

information has been found on it during that time. Shortly before 1900 several books were published on the subject of drawn work. One that should be particularly helpful, if a copy can be found, is *A Treatise on Modern Drawn Work in Color* by Mrs. Isaac Miller Houck of Tiffin, Ohio. It must have been very popular among needleworkers—a second edition was published in 1900. The cost was 75¢.

Recently, a number of turn-of-the-century *Needlecraft* magazines have been found. They contain a wealth of information on all types of needlework and include drawn work. Prices range from a bargain at $1 to an outrageous $9 each. If they can be found, *Home Needlework* magazines, published from 1900 to 1910, are an even better source of information on old needlework.

CHAPTER 10
Art and History of Crochet

There has never been a time since needlework was first developed that it has not been practiced in one form or another. Sometimes one type of needlework will experience greater popularity than another, but invariably the scales will tilt in another direction. Crochet and embroidery always have vied for top honors in the popularity race, and there have been times when it was impossible to tell which, if either, was more popular. At other times they have seemed to be on a seesaw, with one more popular and then the other. Indications are that crochet may be more popular today.

Crocheted items often can be found for

sale at craft shows. The prices on new pieces may occasionally seem a bit high when compared with the old, but prices on the old are rising fast. Generally, the older pieces are more intricately made, but there is also a chance the old crochet will not last as long as the new because it has already given a lifetime of service. Actually, it is surprising how strong the majority of the old pieces are if they have had average care. They may not stand the rough-and-tumble washing machines of today, but then the new crochet shouldn't be subjected to that, either. The biggest problem with old

Wall hanging or pillow top with replica of United States flag.

Butterflies and pansies were crocheted into this antimacassar set.

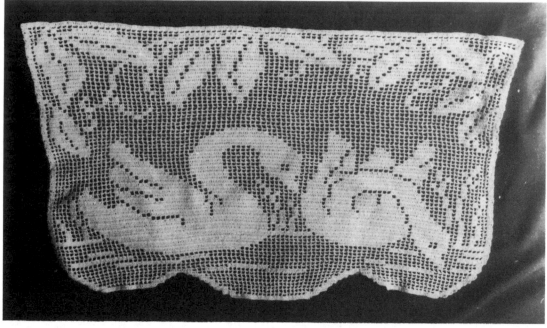

Chair back with swan design.

crochet is broken threads here and there, but even the unskilled worker can take a fine thread and tie the broken places together.

The word "crochet" comes from the French *croches* or *croc* and the old Danish word *krooke,* meaning "hook." It is a simple name for an easy-to-make yet exquisite type of needlework. The only tool required to make crochet is the hook, a handle or stem that can be made of bone, ivory, steel, wood, or tortoiseshell, with a hook on one end. The hook was used to work the balls or hanks of thread into designs that form parts or all of the pieces of crocheted wearing apparel or household linens.

Crochet work was known in Europe as early as the sixteenth century, but like other types of needlework it was practiced mostly by the nuns and workers in the convents. It always has been closely related to lace. In fact, in the early days it was known as nun's lace. During that time it was seldom if ever listed as crochet, and it was lumped into the lace category. The exact date is unknown, but around the

Crocheted basket full of flowers, possibly a chair back.

Front door hanging.

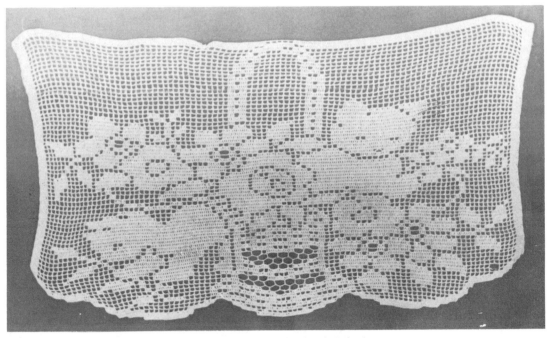

Kittens and basket of flowers make an interesting design for this chair back.

Fraternal order emblems often were crocheted on wall hangings.

This crocheted wall hanging was made after Lindbergh's flight in 1927.

seventeenth century crochet was introduced into Ireland, where they developed it until it was almost as fine as the finest lace. There it became known as Irish point with lace added, naturally.

Crochet might have been developed earlier in Scotland, as there are numerous references to "shepherd's knitting" in the old Scottish Highlands history. Some people think they might have been knitting, while the majority of dedicated needlework researchers believe they were doing some kind of crochet. The reason for that assumption is the fact that several references have been found describing a type of homemade hook, very similar to the crochet hook, that was used to make that particular type of "knitting."

Shortly after 1850 crochet work took England by storm. Credit for developing it into one of the most popular types of needlework in Britain has been given to one woman, Eleanore Reigo de la Branchardiere, daughter of a nobleman of Franco-Spanish descent who fled to England during the French Revolution. She became so engrossed in needlework that she created and introduced intricate designs and patterns and published a monthly magazine and many books, all devoted to needlework and primarily crochet.

With all the interest and publications that developed in England, crochet naturally spread to the colonies. There is little doubt that some type of crocheting had been done earlier in America, probably in the northern states, where it was essential for the family to have heavy woolen garments for the winter. Many of the newcomers probably knew how to crochet and knit, having been taught in their native countries.

Early records mention hooks being used for "looping" wool yarn into various items of clothing. This type of crochet could have been brought over by the Scots, who taught their friends and neighbors "the way they made warm clothing back in the old country."

Shortly after 1850 instructions and discussions on the beauty and "great durability" of crochet work began appearing in books and magazines in America. Those who previously had not known how to crochet learned easily and quickly using the explicit instructions.

In 1858 Mrs. Pullan, while discussing crochet hooks, noted, "None have been found that can be compared, for excellence, with those made by Boulton and Son of Redditch, England. They are numbered from 12 to 24, and one each of Nos. 12, 15, 18, 21, and 24 form an excellent and useful set which will last any careful person a lifetime."

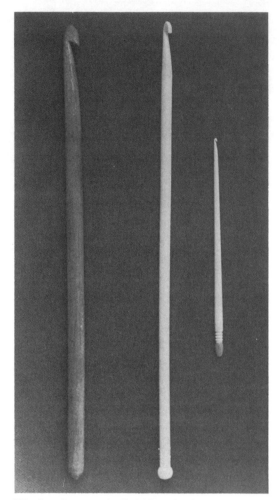

Wooden, ivory, and celluloid crochet hooks.

She went on to give instructions for holding both the thread and the hook. "The crochet needle [apparently crochet hooks were called needles in the beginning] must be held lightly between the forefinger and the thumb of the right hand; the hook horizontal and parallel with the first finger of the left hand, not with the barb pointing upwards or downwards, as is too frequently the case. That work on which you are employed is held closely between the thumb and forefinger of the left hand. The thread crosses the latter and the middle finger which is kept at a little distance; and then is held down by the third finger, close to the middle one. The little finger, only, of the left hand is unemployed."

Pillowcase with small embroidered design and crocheted edging.

Instructions like this were vital on new types of needlework, although in most homes the children began lessons in fancy stitchery when they were very young. In modern society children are seldom if ever taught the fine art of needlework—in great contrast to the old days, when five-year-old girls learned their first stitches on demanding samplers. It might have been a bit early to start lessons, but the parents instilled in their children a sense of accomplishment that made the children want to learn. They were, in most cases, anxious to learn. According to old records, they were delighted with the results.

Incidentally, during the latter part of the nineteenth century some children learned crochet stitches rather than embroidery stitches in their first lessons. Some simply preferred crochet to embroidery, and when they had a choice made rows and rows of crocheted lace or edging to use on pillowcases, dresser scarves, centerpieces, and doilies. Rather than embroidered samplers, many young girls had stacks of household linens. In those days each girl learned all types of needlework, so where she began made little difference. The only thing that was important was that she know them all by the time she really started work on the linens to fill her dower or marriage chest.

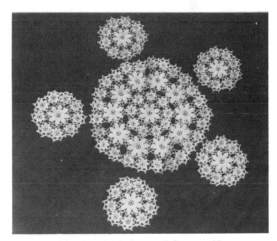

Doilies for lemonade pitcher and five tumblers.

Monogrammed doily for bread tray.

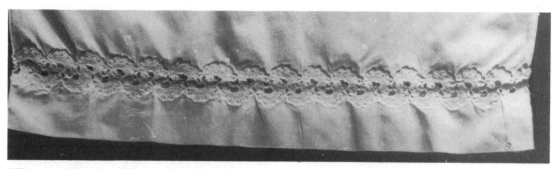

Pillowcase with crocheted insertion.

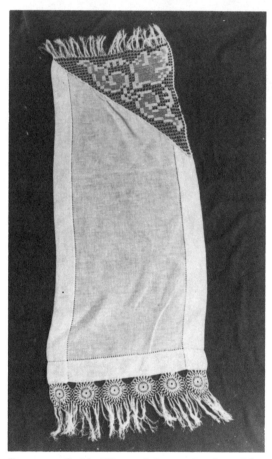

Dresser scarf with different design crocheted on either end.

Oblong crocheted centerpiece.

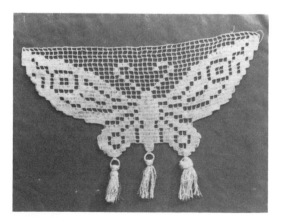

Crocheted end for dresser scarf.

No mothers were as strict or careful in the teaching of their children—not only in the art of needlework but also in the role of the perfect housewife and hostess   as the Danes. It made little difference whether she was a peasant or a princess, her lessons began at age five. These early lessons covered all the simpler stitches and gradually progressed until she could make all stitches in a fine, even stitch. That is one of the reasons the Danes became so famous for the nice details in all their work as well as the exquisite designs where every stitch was made perfectly whether it was embroidery, tatting, knitting, or crochet.

A Danish bride probably had more exquisite linens in her dower or marriage chest than girls from other countries because all her sheets and pillowcases were lavishly embroidered in the finest work and edged with intricate tatting and crochet. Her tablecloths were covered in unrivaled needlework, and she even made curtains that would hang at the windows of either her cottage or castle, depending on birth and luck. She never knew exactly what kind of home she would have after marriage, but as a general rule it would follow the style in which she had grown up. Therefore, she crocheted numerous window panels in what was then called Kensington lace.

Danish mothers were strict about teaching their children all phases of needlework, and so were the schools. Public schools were not as strict as private schools, where there was an unbreakable rule that one hour each day must be spent learning some type of needlework. When the girls arrived home after school, there was another hour of needlework training ("homework"). In Denmark it was essential that everyone keep busy even when visiting. For that reason they invariably carried their needlework when they visited neighbors and family. As they sat chatting, their fingers busily and lovingly continued with their needlework. The bag in which their needlework was carried was itself done entirely in some type of needlework to showcase the ability of the owner.

As in embroidery, the basic or foundation stitch in crochet is the *chain stitch*, sometimes

One of a set of crocheted bullion cup doilies.

Heavy thread was used to make this centerpiece.

Rose bowl doily.

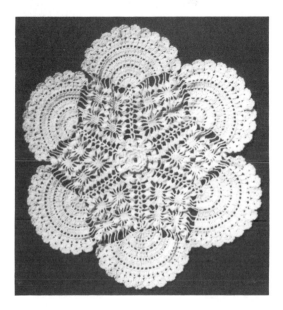

called the tambour stitch by old-timers. Chain stitch in embroidery and crochet were quite similar in that each ended up looking like a chain. The main difference stemmed from the fact that embroidery chain was fastened to the fabric while the crochet chain was simply a row of links or a chain made of thread without benefit of fabric. The other difference is that embroidery is made with a needle while crochet is done with a hook.

Crochet's chain stitch is made by first making a loop near the end of the thread and drawing it up to about the size of the first chain. The hook is inserted into the loop slightly in front of the thread. By a slight movement of the left wrist, the thread is drawn toward the worker and then laid across the hook. The yarn or thread is drawn through the loop and the first chain is made. This stitch can be repeated as many times as necessary. Older workers point out that in making chain stitch, a stitch often used to make plain crocheted rugs, the right hand plays a passive role and the fingers can be held far more gracefully than when making the more intricate stitches. In those days the use of the hands and the graceful way in which they were held was extremely important.

In instructions and directions crochet stitches are abbreviated to include only a few letters. Chain stitch is simply "ch."

Braid chain stitch was described as one that made a pretty braid "of the kind usually called Grecian plait." It was touted as useful for many purposes, but instructions for only one (a pen wiper) were given. To make this braid one made two chain stitches and then inserted the hook in the first one without taking it from the loop already on the hook. Then the next loop was brought through both. After this first intricate stitch, the hook always was inserted in the last stitch and the thread drawn through it together with the one already on the hook.

In some pieces braids similar to those used to make Battenberg and other braid laces were used with crochet. In this case the braids were crocheted together with different patterns and designs rather than worked together with different types of needlework like the Battenbergs. Apparently, this work was not too popular as little has been seen and only a few instructions found.

Double crochet, known as "dc," is quite similar to short double crochet, and the work is begun in the same way. When the loops are all on the hook, the thread is only drawn through two of them, leaving one beside the new stitch. The next stitch is worked the same way, leaving one loop with the new stitch. Since two loops are used each time, it seems appropriate that it was called double crochet.

In later years *rickrack* replaced braids as makers crocheted all types of edging. For wider rows of edging two or three rows of rickrack might be used; for the narrow only one row. In a few instances doilies and centerpieces were completely made of rows of rickrack crocheted together. As late as 1950 some magazines were giving instructions for this work. A favorite for edging at that time was pastel-colored rickrack crocheted with white thread. Early on the women had crocheted coronation braids into designs to make edgings and insertions. Now they simply were substituting rickrack for the coronation braid.

To make *short double crochet,* identified as "sdc," the worker puts the thread around the hook before inserting it into the stitch that is to be worked. The thread is then drawn through the stitch, making two loops on the hook, and the thread is passed around between them. The thread is then drawn through all three at once.

One crochet writer, who claimed credit for creating or inventing the *short treble crochet* stitch in the 1850s, described it this way: "Put the thread twice around the needle before inserting the hook in the stitch to be worked. Having drawn the thread through the latter, you have what is equal to four loops on the needle, draw the thread through two and then through the remaining two and the loop just made, together." This stitch is shown as "stc" in instructions.

Single crochet, known as "sc," is made by having a loop on the hook and then inserting the hook in a stitch and drawing the thread through the loop. The thread is again put over the hook and brought through two loops.

Slip stitch, identified in instructions as "sl,"

is made by keeping the loop that is already on the hook and inserting the hook in the stitch and drawing the thread through both at the same time.

The writer's description of *treble crochet* was equally interesting. To make treble crochet, she wrote, "Begin like the last, but draw the thread through two loops only at a time, and as it will take you three times to do it, the stitch is called treble crochet."

Other stitches known to have been used by the early crocheters were ribbed crochet, crochet cross-stitch, Princess Fredricka William stitch, picot, open and open-raised tricot, point de tricot, and Josephine tricot stitch. Most of them had variations like raised, long, or cross-treble stitch.

Types of crochet were as varied as those in other types of needlework.

Bead crochet was popular for more than fifty years. Among the many items made of bead crochet were opera glass bags; reticules (also known as purses, pocketbooks, or handbags); and some pieces of jewelry. The reticule or purse was a late bloomer. Ladies previously had little or nothing to take with them except a handkerchief, which they usually carried in their hands. Suddenly, milady was not fashionable if she did not have a reticule or handbag for all occasions. The correct size for this dainty bag was described as "of sufficient size to carry one's handkerchief and opera glasses, and if need be, will accommodate other articles as well." It soon becomes very obvious that those ladies who made crocheted beaded bags were more dedicated than most. That realization comes with reading the first line of instructions for making one. "String colored beads," it read, "as follows: 520 white, 1 bronze, 70 white, 3 bronze, 70 white, and 2 bronze." Now this was only one line in six pages of instructions for making one bag. The tiniest of tiny beads were being used.

Like most things in those days, especially those used in needlework, the price of the beads were very reasonable. They were so small nobody counted until they began stringing. For that reason they were advertised and sold by the "bunch," with a bunch costing 10¢. That price was for crystal beads, the most popular at the time (probably due to the price). Gold beads were much more expensive, with forty cents being the average price. Bugle beads sold for about the same price as the gold. Prices rose somewhat when buying larger beads or those made to imitate pearls, coral, turquoise, or amethyst. These were counted and sold for approximately 3¢ to 4¢ a dozen.

Calling cards were an important part of social life during the Victorian era and were used well into this century. On the days she was "at home," the lady of the house welcomed guests, but on other days she went to call on the ones who had called on her previously. She might drive her own carriage or have a servant drive it, depending on her station in life. Visiting and being visited was a never-ending cycle. One of the requirements of such visitation was leaving a calling card. This custom is responsible for two of our most treasured antiques: the calling card tray (made of china, silver, or glass), and the calling card case. The case was used to carry several calling cards in the event that she found several people not at home. The calling card case could be made of gold, silver, tortoiseshell, or mother-of-pearl or it could be handmade by the owner in bead crochet. Once the reticule or purse became popular, calling cards were carried in it.

Probably the best way for today's collectors to identify the crocheted beaded bag is to remember most of the early bags were only beaded on one side. Later they would be beaded on both sides, which made them more attractive. These bags also were called chatelaine bags. At first the circular shape was the most popular, then it was discovered they could be made in any shape or size. Directions and photographs of opera glass bags show most of them without handles but with expandable tops. The miser's purse, seldom done in crocheted beadwork, always was divided into two separate compartments divided by a ring that could be pushed either way. There was also a clutch- or envelope-type purse that is easily distinguished from the calling card case because it is three or four times larger.

In 1900 one needlework authority in *Home Needlework Magazine* described the floral drawstring purse she had designed: "This

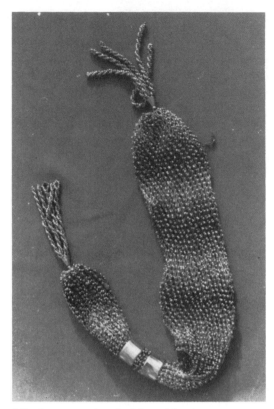

Crocheted drawstring purse.

Miser's purse crocheted with steel beads.

quaint bag is a [survivor] of an ancient pattern and forms an excellent illustration of the type now so popular in reticules—bags carried upon the arm or by the cord or ribbon by which they are drawn and fastened." The bag to be done in beaded crochet had loops around the sides to hold the drawstring.

Decor crochet was neither very widely used nor very well known if one has to judge by the pieces found today. They are extremely scarce, and this could be due to the fact that decor crochet was used more on clothing than on household linens. Unfortunately, clothing was not preserved like the linens. Decor was simple, beautiful, and not too expensive to make, but its uses were limited. It was especially decorative and beautiful on wedding dresses.

In decor crochet the worker covered a small transparent form with plain crochet. The forms came in four sizes. The largest (No. 1), called the oval form, measured one inch on the outside at the longest point. The second largest

(No. 2) measured three-quarters of an inch long. The third (No. 3) was round and three-quarters of an inch in diameter. The smallest (No. 4) was one-half-inch round and was called the jewel. After the crocheting was completed, all the forms except the smallest one were filled with a network of silk threads. This work was done from the wrong side, and the silk thread was placed from side to side at even distances until the center was well filled. The crochet-covered forms then were basted on a pattern on the fabric where the connecting lines of the design could be worked in Roman floss. After the outlining was completed, the forms were sewn to the fabric using plain cotton sewing thread.

Instructions have been found for making a wedding dress that, according to the directions, can become just a dressy dress once the ceremony is over. A list of the materials required for the dress and their costs show that in 1905 this wedding dress could be made for $14.72. Eight yards of bobbinet (fabric) two

Directions for this filet crochet were given in a 1923 Needlecraft Magazine.

Butterflies were popular with Victorian crocheters and were used on this serving tray cover.

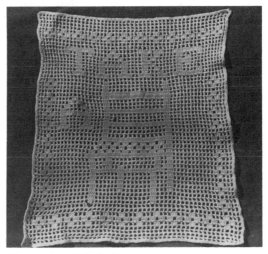

Filet crochet chair back.

yards wide could be bought for $10. Thread required for the crocheting and embroidery was thirty-eight skeins of Persian floss, ten skeins of Roman floss, and seven skeins of Filo silk for a total cost of $2.20. Decor forms to be covered in crochet included twenty-one packages of No. 2, nine of No. 3, four of No. 4, and two of No. 1, for a total cost of $2.52.

One of the most popular types of crochet was *filet crochet,* and many pieces in this work still can be found today. The charm of filet crochet lies in the sentiments expressed in the sayings and one-liners that ranged from local quotables to Shakespeare and Burns. Although many of the pieces have only the profile of a woman or a basket of flowers, the majority

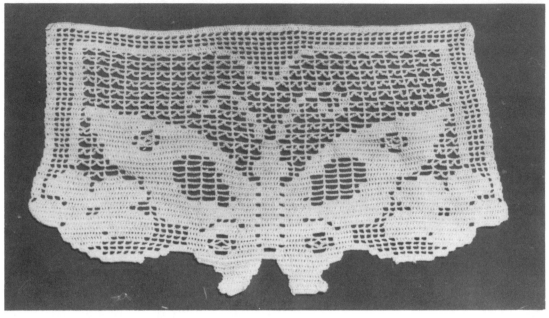

One of a pair of crocheted ends for a dresser scarf.

have quaint lines and objects in lieu of some words. For instance, a cover for rolls had the words "hot rolls make the" and a magnificent butterfly in filet crochet. An antimacassar had the words "Take a" and the silhouette of a chair. One old tablecloth has a four-line welcome in filet crochet, with one line in each corner. The first line is "Freely welcome to my cup," then "May'st thou sit and sip it up," the third is "Make the most of life you may," and the fourth "Life is short and fades away."

Much filet crochet was being made as late as 1920, and one needleworker remembers this as the time when long scarves that had been so popular for use on sideboards and long tables were being replaced by shorter scarves or three matching rectangular pieces. Since there were no standard sizes, these pieces easily could be confused with the "tea cart cover," a piece made either in crochet or a combination of needleworks made especially for the tea cart. Each worker made the short scarf according to the size of her sideboard and serving tray. Most were made with fabric centers and inserts or borders in filet crochet. One of the new designs

popular then was a scarf made with a fabric center that had apple tree branches crocheted in a design on either end and the sentiment "A dinner of herbs—among friends" crocheted on the front edging.

Embroidered tea cart cover with crocheted border.

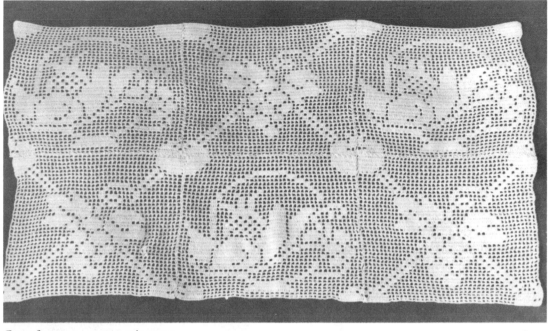

Cover for a tea cart or serving tray.

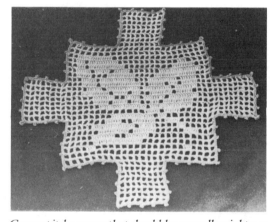

Cream pitcher cover that should have small weights on each corner.

Crocheted cover for a hot dish (asbestos) mat.

Collars, cuffs, and belts were crocheted with a filet floral design and open work for running ribbons through the sides or center.

It is believed that the later *Irish crochet* was in reality a poorer version of the fine *Irish point crochet* made during the seventeenth century. During the nineteenth century the quality of all needlework declined somewhat because the average housewife, who made most of the needlework at that time, did not have unlim-

ited hours to spend on her needlework. So she cut out a troublesome stitch here and a fancy design there and converted it to the less-complicated patterns and designs that were more in keeping with everyday household use. Very likely that is what happened to the ultra-fine Irish point—not only was part of the name omitted, but some of the intricacy went as well.

Irish crochet, often referred to as Irish lace, is one of the most durable and beautiful

More than likely this pair was used as covers for some type of serving tray.

Crocheted cuffs for a dress or jacket.

Collar in Irish crochet.

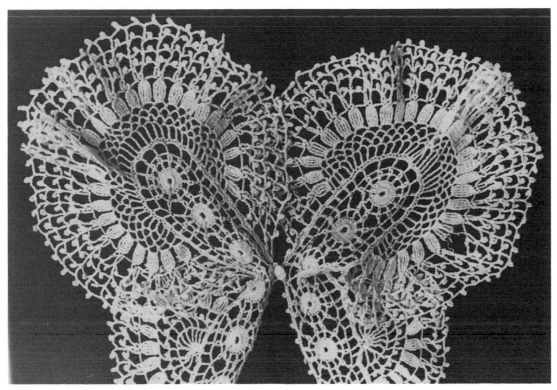

Jabot was crocheted on the end of the collar.

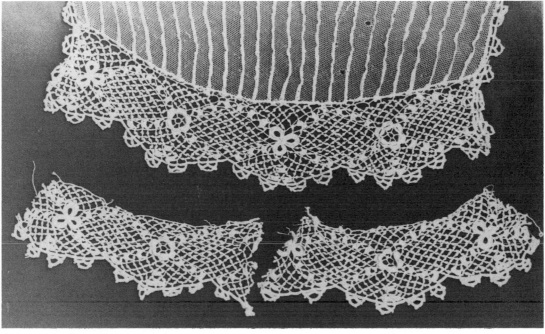

Collar and cuff set in Irish crochet.

types of crochet. It was used on everything from kimonos to wedding dresses, and was one of the few types of crochet that survived repeated washings and remained fresh and pretty. One of the secrets of that freshness was in the correct ironing process. It stayed fresh and pretty if it was lightly starched and then ironed on a heavy blanket after each washing.

While some of the most beautiful pieces of Irish crochet were too intricate for the average worker, there still were many pretty designs that could be made by workers with only average ability. The plainest of Irish crochet was considered intricate when compared to most types of crochet because the motifs and figures were made separately and then crocheted together. First the motifs were made, and then basted in place on a thin paper pattern that already had been basted over a foundation of at least four thicknesses of newspaper or other pliable paper. Then and only then could the background or filling be crocheted, with the motifs and figures joined together with rows of picot loops. As late as the 1940s, ladies' gloves were made of crocheted picot loops with Irish crochet flowers tacked on the top.

Since the motifs or floral designs in Irish crochet were done separately, it was perfect for making artificial flowers of the kind that were used so extensively in corsages. They also were used to decorate milady's gorgeous hats and on photo frames, fire screens, lamp shades, and for household adornments such as table decorations. These dainty flowers also were used on clothing, especially little girls' dress collars. Called *Irish floral crochet,* it was not as easy to make as ordinary crochet, but was well worth the extra effort as it could be used on wearing apparel or displayed in the home to give the worker that wonderful opportunity to show off her work—unpretentiously.

The first step in making the Irish floral crochet was to try to match the color of the silk crochet thread as nearly as possible to the natural color of the flower to be made. The stems and edges of the petals were worked around or over a fine wire on the same order as decor crochet. For larger flowers a strong wire was needed, and for this the workers used the

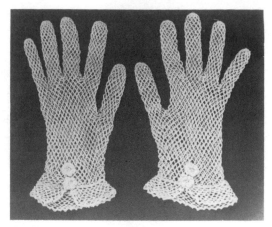

Crocheted gloves with Irish floral crochet at top.

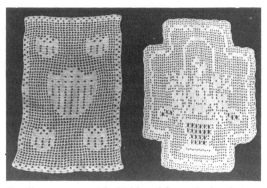

Small tray covers with shield and flower basket designs.

stiff wire generally used at that time by milliners for holding wide hat brims in shape. The smaller wire was the same type as that used by florists. Only the most experienced workers could make the smaller flowers like the primulas (primrose), myosotis (forget-me-not), and cineraria (a small daisylike flower) as the thread used to make them was as fine as sewing thread. Some actually used sewing thread when making Irish floral crochet. This in turn required a crochet hook large enough to take the silk thread without cutting it yet one that was small enough to make close, even stitches.

Although crochet as we know it was a late bloomer in the field of needlework, some have tried to prove that it was one of the earlier types made. In fact, this could be true since very few

Centerpiece with border in relief crochet.

Unusual centerpiece with appliquéd embroidered butterfly and relief crochet border.

Close-up of relief crochet.

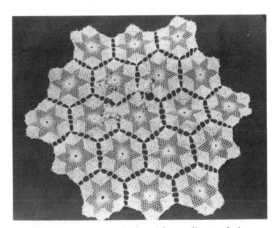

Damaged centerpiece made with small star design.

explicit records have been found of the actual types of needlework. It is often described vaguely—as it is in the Bible, where mention is made of the Israelites making and using gold thread. We can reasonably assume they made some type of embroidery, yet gold thread always has been associated with the bullion stitch. Hence, when relief crochet made its appearance, there were those who tried to give it an ancient heritage.

Relief crochet differs from other types of crochet in several ways. The crochet hook is held in the hand rather than between the

thumb and forefinger, as it is when making most types of crochet. In most types of crochet, the thread is seldom wrapped around the hook more than three or four times, yet in relief crochet it could be wrapped around as many as twenty times depending on the size "roll" needed for that particular pattern. In most types of needlework it behooves the worker to search for a needle that will carry thread without cutting it, and the size of the hook can vary as much as three numbers. In relief crochet the correct size is absolutely essential if the work is to be perfect. The best way to choose the

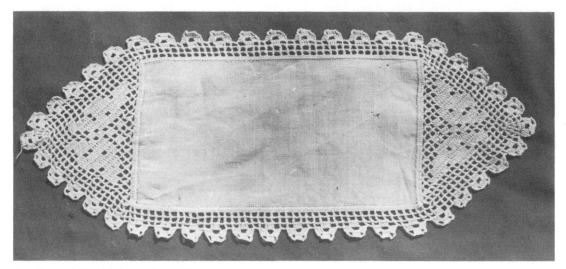

Bread tray doily with butterfly motif.

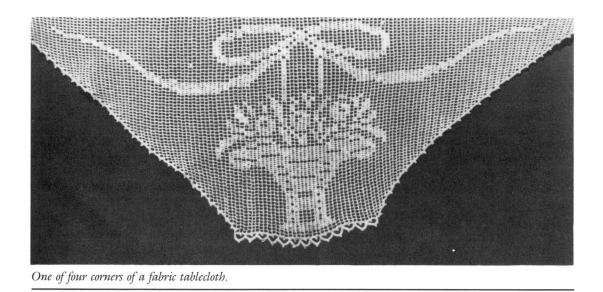

One of four corners of a fabric tablecloth.

perfect size is to select one where the hook is just filled by the size of thread that would be used. It also is considered helpful to run the silk back and forth over the hook. If the fibers of the silk catch on it, the hook is too small. If the hook is too large, it will be difficult to pull it through the coil.

Roll stitch was the basic stitch in relief crochet. Other relief crochet stitches included rose stitch, roll picot, rose treble, Russian spoke, and Russian picot spoke stitch.

Like all types of crochet, relief work could be used in many ways. It could be used to make a complete centerpiece or doily or edging for a piece with a fabric center. It was found that it was best to use fabric centers on large pieces like scarves or large centerpieces. It was also less expensive, as relief crochet usually was made with silk thread (although cotton and linen were used later). Grandmother found that relief crochet was very impressive when used on collars; cuffs; yokes; belts; revers

Pointed yoke for camisole or corset cover.

(lapels); vest fronts; fancy bonnet crowns; shopping bags; reticules or purses; watch guards; trim for lingerie; and passementerie for capes, dresses, and jackets.

Other than the small number of embroidered cases for shirts, detachable collars, cuffs, and cigars, there were few needlework items that appealed to men or could be used by them. In crochet, however, there was one that apparently became extremely popular: the crocheted silk four-in-hand tie. It was described in glowing terms as early as 1905, and by 1908 *Home Needlework Magazine* stated, "There has been nothing this season in neckwear quite so popular with the well-dressed man as the crocheted silk tie." There were complaints that the handmade ties were selling for as much as $3 each at fine haberdashers, but the skilled wife or girlfriend could make one for less than 50¢. Most were made with the simplest crochet stitches using nothing but the finest silk thread. Reasons for using silk were twofold. First, the tie was worn around the neck where it was easily seen, and the ladies were always careful with items that would reflect on their ability as homemakers.

Fabric centerpiece with wide crocheted border.

Unless the best silk was used, the tie might become shapeless or stretchy. Workers also had to be careful to make good, firm stitches, as that was one deterrent to shapelessness and stretching. All ties first were made in navy blue, plum, and dark green. Then, as their popularity grew, Corticelli introduced a new crochet silk called "Tieknit" that produced a variegated effect.

Perhaps one of the reasons for the popularity of crochet was and still is the fact it can be made with any type of thread, from fine sewing thread to heavy yarn. Fine thread has been used to make everything from tiny medallions on baby layettes to centerpieces, while heavy yarn was used to make wearing apparel that ranged from gloves to shawls. Nearly everything that could be made in embroidery or decorated with embroidery could be done in crochet. Many towels and splashers will be found with crocheted edging and insertions, but none will be found made entirely of crochet, as that was not feasible. Crocheted napkin rings were made in much larger numbers than the embroidered ones, probably because they were prettier and showed up better on the fabric napkins.

A good amount of skirts and dresses have been crocheted through the years, but the majority of crocheted wearing apparel consists of hats, shawls, house slippers or shoes, vests, jackets, and gloves. Some of the most beautiful blouses and jackets were made of a combination of Irish crochet and embroidered fabric panels. Baby layettes usually included several crocheted caps, sacques, booties, and blankets. One of the more popular unseen items was the crocheted yoke for chemises and corset covers. A crocheted yoke also was made for nightgowns.

There still is an abundance of old crocheted tablecloths and bedspreads, but not everyone wants to use them today as such, nor

Both pieces of a crocheted yoke for a nightgown.

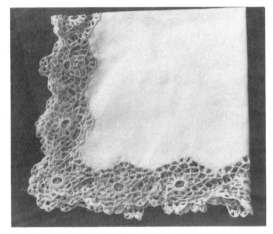

Handkerchief with crocheted edging.

Crocheted boudoir cap.

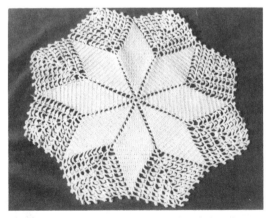

Around 1900 this was a very popular design for centerpieces.

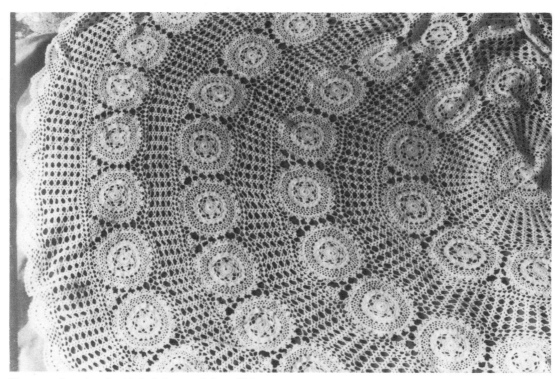

New round crocheted tablecloth imported from China.

Doily for pickle dish.

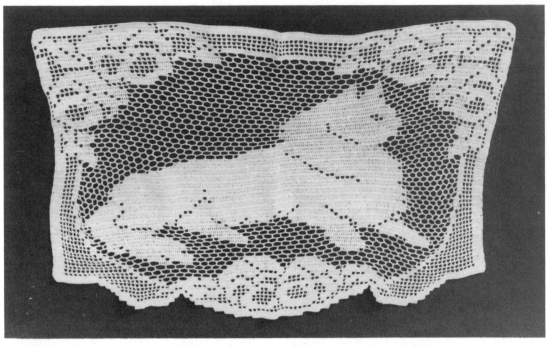

Reclining cat decorates this crocheted chair back.

Antimacassar set with dog design.

does everybody want to use old crocheted centerpieces and doilies. But the uses being found for some of those old pieces makes one wonder if the descendants aren't more ingenious than the people who originally made the pieces. Some still use the pieces as grandmother did, with the centerpiece on tables and the crocheted bedspreads on modern beds. Another group is restoring old log and Victorian houses, filling them with antiques, and using the household linens as they were originally. A third group is the most ingenious. They are devising new ways to use old needlework that are not only beautiful but also differ-

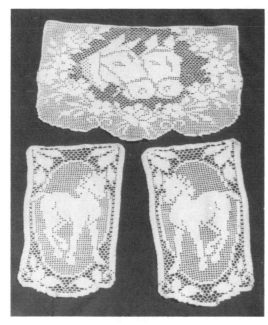

Antimacassar set with horse design.

Crocheted basket starched stiff enough to stand.

Wall hanging or pillow top with peacock design.

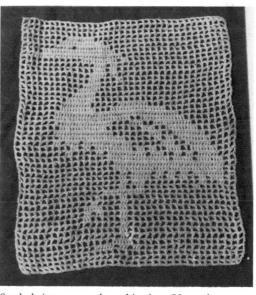

Stork design was used on this piece. Use unknown.

ent—like the young mother who used a loosely crocheted bedspread as a canopy cover for her daughter's bed. There is still another group of needlework collectors who collect for the sheer joy of owning handmade items that are so intricate and so beautiful.

Scarce old handmade wooden hooks are highly sought after. Most of the old ones of any kind have disappeared, but now and then some will be found in an old sewing box or basket at an estate sale. The majority were made in one piece, but there were some hooks with fancy handles that fastened onto a short hook. Nearly a century ago one company offered hooks in sets, where one handle would fit the various hooks in the set. Those who can remember say the sets weren't very satisfactory. Most workers, it seems, preferred the one-

piece hook, which accounts for the scarcity of sets today. Beautiful cases—some embroidered, some crocheted—were made to hold the worker's hooks. Generally they were more popular in England than in the United States.

There is still a plentiful supply of gorgeous crochet pieces available in antiques shops and shows as well as the malls. Some good ones have been found recently in the larger flea markets. Apparently the growing interest in all types of needlework is responsible for the large selection.

CHAPTER 11
Easy and Inexpensive Hairpin Work

Which name do you prefer—hairpin crochet or hairpin lace? There has been controversy through the years over the different names, as one group has adamantly called it hairpin crochet while the other, equally as firm, refers to it only as hairpin lace. Old references and instructions have been equally divided in the use of the name. In order to stay in the middle, it is referred to here as hairpin work. Actually either name would be correct because it does become a flimsy, lacy type of work in the end and it is made with a crochet hook.

Generally hairpin work was made as an edging, but doilies and centerpieces made entirely of hairpin work are rather plentiful. It was called hairpin crochet or lace because it was made on an old-fashioned hairpin. Plain or straight hairpins were most recommended, but the kinky kind was used when nothing else was available. Hairpin work didn't necessarily have to be made on a hairpin, as there were several factory-made tools especially for use in making hairpin work called forks or staples. The forks or staples were made in several sizes to accommodate coarse or fine work. Few bought them, preferring instead to use "the tools at hand"—the hairpin. It also was less expensive to use the hairpin. Instructions and directions packaged with the fork or staple naturally mentioned the hairpin, but the instructions found in old needlework books and magazines specified it.

Some went a step further and devised other methods for making hairpin work. Those wanting larger loops than could be made on a hairpin used a pair of knitting needles. They could be fastened at one end by whatever method the owner could devise. If the owner was lucky enough to have a husband who whittled, he would more than likely whittle out a wooden gadget to hold the knitting needles a correct distance apart. The work was done on the knitting needles exactly as it was on the hairpin, but the loops were much larger.

No matter how you view it, hairpin work was neither as intricate nor as tedious as crochet or tatting. In fact, it was a poor substitute, but it was easy and inexpensive to make and it worked up quickly. One of the reasons it was so inexpensive was that this gave the worker a chance to use up that partial hank of

Hairpin lace doily with crocheted center.

143

thread left over from another project. There always were crochet hooks in her sewing basket and hairpins in her hair, so she didn't have to spend a penny. The work is pretty and different, but it is not nearly as pretty as regular crochet. In most of the work regular crochet was added to make the hairpin work more attractive.

The work could be made with the prongs of the hairpin pointing up or down; it all depended on the preference of the worker, as each had its advantages and disadvantages. Working with the prongs down meant the crocheting had to be done near the curve or end of the hairpin, which meant the crochet hook had to be removed each time the pin was turned. But on the other hand, there was the advantage of slipping off the end of long strips without removing all the work from the hairpin. When working with the prongs pointing up, the crocheting was done near the points so the pin could be turned and the hook lifted over the points without having to remove it completely. Likely each worker settled into the habit of turning the pin in the direction it was pointed when she learned to do hairpin work.

The work was seldom, if ever, used just as it came off the hairpin. It was combined with regular crochet to form strips or rosettes. Work that was well done would have loops that were uniform in size, and this was no easy chore when you think of the flexibility of a hairpin. If the strip of uniform loops was long enough, it could be worked together so that simple crochet could be attached to one side, leaving the other plain to be whipped on pillow cases and napkins.

Another way to use hairpin work was to make rosettes. To form the rosettes one had to fasten off after sixteen loops were made on either side, then another sixteen would be made. This continued for as many rosettes as were required. One side of the section of loops was tied together to form a center. After several of them were made they were enhanced with a crocheted foundation made of two rows of double square crochet, with four to six of the loops in each rosette being caught in the foundation.

Fabric center with hairpin work border.

Earlier the favorite thread for making hairpin work was silk, but cotton soon replaced it. Linen thread was used but not frequently. To make a very fine edging some workers used regular sewing thread, but it was so fine that it was extremely tedious to work with. From the beginning it seemed to be the custom to use whatever thread was available. Since hairpin work required less thread than regular crochet, workers often used up leftovers. This could have been part of the appeal of hairpin work: It could be made from leftovers, which meant it didn't cost anything, and it was made with tools already in the sewing basket.

To make hairpin lace one began by making a loop in the thread and slipping it over one of the prongs (these instructions are for making it with the prongs down). Turning the hairpin around, the crochet hook was placed under the thread and the thread was drawn through. Then a double crochet stitch was made over all the threads between the prongs. The hook was removed from the loop, the hairpin turned, and the hook reinserted in the loop. Again the thread was drawn through and another double crochet stitch was made. This process continued until the required number of loops had been made. The hairpin always was turned from right to left, but the type of stitches could vary.

In the 1940s this idea was revised. The

144

hairpin was replaced by a small wooden frame called an E-Z-Duz-It crochet frame, which sold for one dollar. However, the idea of two small, round pieces about the size of a pencil with a bar across each end was so simple that many workers made their own using regular dowels and bar closures. At least two instruction booklets were published describing the method as "a fascinating new method for making afghans, baby carriage robes, rugs, sweaters, moccasins, shoulderettes [a modern version of the shawl], and baby garments." They claimed a full-sized afghan could be made in thirty-six hours, a sweater in five hours.

Evidently it was not only a speedy process but it also was much less expensive than regular crochet, as only three 4-ounce skeins of yarn were required for the sweater. The frame, measuring just a little over a foot long, was much larger than the old hairpin, and most of the items made on it were to use wool yarn. There were directions for making a ribbon blouse, which must have been expensive since 1150 yards of what they called dress ribbon were required to make it. Instructions were given for making doilies and place mats using heavy cotton crochet thread. The same stitches were used on this work as on the earlier hairpin work.

It is possible that some of the old forks or

Combination of drawn work and hairpin work.

staples still can be found, or some collectors already may have some in their collections of needlework. When found, these are the only hairpin crochet- or lace-related antiques known (unless one wants to include the crochet hook and the hairpin). A great deal of the work is available. Pieces can be found in any pile of old linens. So far, prices have been very reasonable.

CHAPTER 12
The Simplicity of Tatting

"Never was tatting more in favor than at the present time, indeed, the shuttle fairly rivals the crochet hook as an implement for weaving webs of gossamer," wrote one needleworker in 1915. At that time tatting had been in favor in some countries for nearly 200 years, but like all types of needlework it had faded in and out of popularity.

It is generally believed that tatting originated in Italy during the seventeenth century; as with most arts, crafts, and needlework, no records were kept, therefore dating it exactly is impossible.

Knotting was more popular outside of Italy, nevertheless it is believed that tatting was simply an extension or variation of the old knotting. The big difference between the two was the way such pieces were used and the size of the shuttles used to make them. Knotting was applied to the fabric in a type of appliquéd decoration while tatting, in the early days, was used for edging lace. In fact, there are those who say that tatting is only a reproduction of the ragusa gimp laces, and to this day tatting often is referred to as lace and sometimes as tatted lace.

The shuttles used to make knotting were rather large, usually between one and two inches in width and four to six inches long, while the tatting shuttle was seldom an inch wide, with three-quarters of an inch the most popular size. None were over four inches long.

Although there are few records of the work done early in the nineteenth century, there are plenty from the later years as tatting blossomed in many countries around 1850.

Credit for that goes to Eleanore Reigo de la Blanchardiere, who did so much to spread the word about all types of needlework, especially crochet. In England she combined her talents with Therese de Dillmont to publicize the beauty and durability of tatting.

In America one of the early leaders of the tatting school was a Mrs. Pullan (no first name was given), whose *The Lady's Manual of Fancy Work* was published in 1858. In the section on tatting she said that she felt it should have been more popular than it was, indicating that it already was well known. She admitted it could not be done in "such an infinite variety of patterns as knitting and crochet, but those that

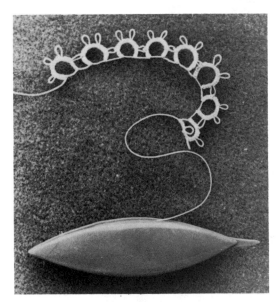

Celluloid shuttle with tatting in progress.

146

Metal shuttle.

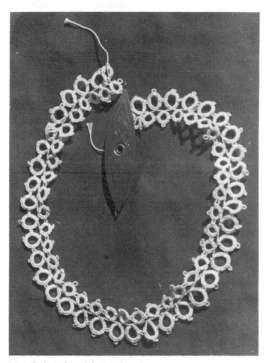

Metal shuttle with tatting in progress.

and celluloid. Some of the early shuttles were handmade as gifts for loved ones, and they were works of art—especially the ivory ones carved by sailors on seagoing vessels. Others were made by people skilled in work with stones and gold. Some were so exquisite that they could be classed as fine jewelry. One of those specially made shuttles had the owner's initials set in garnets on a rock crystal ground and mounted in gold. Many were filagreed and some had precious stones here and there, but few had the owner's initials set in precious or semiprecious stones.

The tatting shuttle can best be described as an elongated tool on which the thread was wound and then worked over and under in circles. As the work progressed, specific amounts of thread were released to make the lace, or as was said, "weave webs of gossamer."

The shuttle was made of two oval pieces flat on the inside and convex on the outside. They were held together at just the right distance by a reel, sometimes round but often oblong, in the center. The thread was wound on this reel before the work began, and as it progressed, the thread was reeled off a few turns at a time until it was all used. It then was refilled and the work continued. To join new thread onto the work, the worker tied both pieces together with a weaver's knot at the base of a loop.

If you want to try to collect only the old shuttles, one of the best ways to tell the old ones from the newer shuttles is by the pinheads that will show on either side of the reel. Two brass pins, placed through the sides of the shuttle on either side of the reel, were used on the very early specimens to hold them together. Early tatters had to be extremely careful in the selection of their shuttles, as those with pins slightly protruding could be aggravating if not downright harmful to the thread. They had a tendency to catch on it with each stitch.

The only other tool necessary for tatting was the so-called pin and ring. The pin, with a slight hook on the end, was attached to one end of a short chain while a ring was attached to the other end of the chain. The ring was worn on the little finger of the right hand so the pin could be used without removing the ring

are made in it are, at once, strong and handsome." She suggested it was a type of needlework that was particularly suitable for elderly people and invalids as it "was so easy to execute and requires only simple tools."

Tools for tatting were very simple, as only a shuttle was necessary; but at that time tatters felt a pin and ring were helpful. Of course, balls or hanks of thread in the correct size were absolutely essential.

During the years shuttles have been made of various materials such as ivory, imitation ivory, bone, gold, silver, tortoiseshell, amber, mother-of-pearl, woods finished in lacquer or after the Vernis Martin style, and later metals

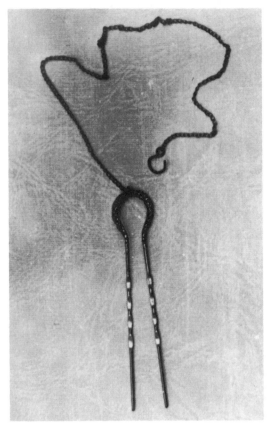

Gold-plated hairpin from eyeglasses, often used when tatting.

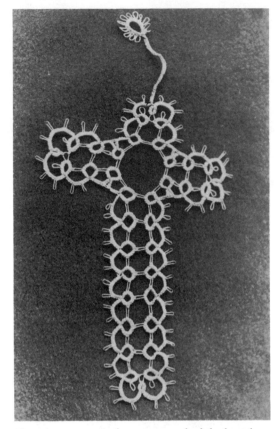

Tatted cross was made as a prayer book bookmark.

from the finger. Originally, the pin was used to make the purls or picots, but later it was found it could be extremely helpful in drawing loops up so they could be connected to the various parts of the design. This exact tool was not absolutely necessary since any type of pin would serve the same purpose; this one was just more convenient to use.

Later the ladies would use the gold hairpin that was attached to the small chain on their glasses. There was always some question as to whether those little gold hairpins were serviceable or even necessary with the eyeglasses or mere window dressing. In the case of tatters it made little difference. Regardless of their original use, they became a marvelous tool for the tatters, and some who didn't even wear glasses bought them and wore them on their "shirtwaist," where they were easy to find and use as their nimble fingers plied the shut-

tle. Much later the shuttles would have a small point on one end that would take the place of the pin.

Tatting was and is a simple process if one works the thread correctly, because it is all in the movement of the fingers and hand. The correct movement makes a stitch while an incorrect one only makes a knot that is almost impossible to remove.

Old instructions describe the tatting stitch being made with a two-part movement. The shuttle is held lightly between the thumb and first or second finger of the right hand. Taking the thread, a few inches from the end, between the thumb and forefinger of the left hand, the worker carries it around the other fingers (that should be held slightly apart) and back again to the thumb, where it is held between it and the forefinger. Then with a slight, sudden movement of the right hand, the tatter throws the thread that goes between it and the left hand over the knuckles of the left hand and passes the shuttle up under the loop around the fingers and above the thread around the knuckles. She then draws the shuttle to the right with a slight jerk, keeping the thread in an even, horizontal line and at the same time contracting the fingers on the left hand to slacken the thread over them. This forms a slipknot on the thread. With the slightest wrong movement in this final operation, the worker can make a nasty little knot, but with the right movement it will become a beautiful slipknot.

This is the first half of the tatting stitch. For the second half the thread is dropped in front of the work instead of throwing it over the hand, and the shuttle is inserted from the back under the loops that are over the fingers. The shuttle is drawn through and the stitch is finished as in the first half of the stitch.

The first part of the stitch is called a half stitch while both are known as a double stitch. This is, of course, the basic tatting stitch. There are only two others that are well known: the purl (or picot) and Josephine knot.

Josephine knot is a knot stitch used as an ornament to break the line of a straight piece of thread when the work is only being done with one thread. The Josephine knot is made by making a loop, then working five to seven half stitches into it. The number of stitches is determined by the size of the thread being used. As the loop is being drawn up and just before it is completely drawn, the shuttle is put through it. By drawing it tightly a large knot will be formed.

In the early days it was generally called a purl, but in later years it became known as a picot. The loops made by the double stitch were joined to each other by picots. Since this is the place where the old pin and ring played such an important role, it probably will be best to quote the old instructions verbatim. In 1858 Mrs. Pullan described the making of picots.

Loops are joined to each other by means of a picot. It is to make these that the pin and chain or pin and ring are required. These pins may be of silver, with a chain about three inches long and a ring large enough to slip over the thumb; but a large rug needle in which coarse thread is knotted, with a loop at the end, for the thumb, will answer the same purpose. A sharp needle is unfit for this purpose. For coarse work, one of the large pins, called blanket pins, is excellent. Having attached the pin to the thumb of the left hand, where it hangs down ready for use, do the first stitch or stitches of the loop. When the picot is to be made lay the point of the needle above and parallel with those stitches, close to them and before making the next, pass the thread already around the fingers over the pin. Go on with the stitches without moving the pin, laying the thread over it as often as a picot is to be made. When the loop is finished, withdraw the pin or needle and draw it up. Picots are sometimes made merely for ornaments.

According to later instructions the picots were used solely for ornaments. The pin, if one was available, was used to pull threads through close places. The first instructions were written several hundred years ago, but it is interesting to note that as time passed many new ideas and some shortcuts were developed in all types of needlework, including tatting. Yet the stitches and the principle remained the same.

Tatting was known and practiced the world over. In other countries it was known by different names. In France it was called *fravolite,* a name used quite often in the early days in both France and America. In Italy, where it is believed to have originated, it was called *occhi;* in most Oriental countries it was known as *makouk.*

In crochet and knitting each stitch is slightly dependent on the others. If one is broken or becomes unfastened, it endangers the others, as they may unravel or be pulled out. In tatting each stitch stands on its own. The way tatted stitches are made causes each to be a more-or-less separate stitch that is difficult to undo and almost impossible to ravel out. Although the lacy tatted pieces look similar to crochet and knitting, if just a bit more fragile, they actually are much stronger.

At first tatting only was used to make edgings, using fine thread for handkerchiefs, baby dresses, and caps and coarser thread for

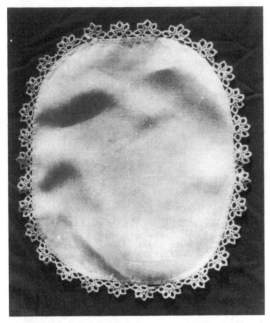

Centerpiece with tatted edging made with heavy thread.

Centerpiece embroidered in silk thread with wide row of tatted edging.

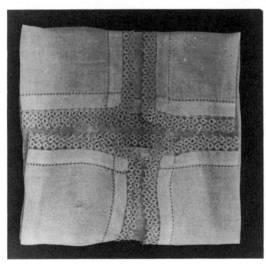

Handkerchief with edging made of fine thread.

Napkin with row of tatting.

edgings on pillowcases, towels, petticoats, centerpieces, and doilies. Even the coarse threads used in tatting were considered fine when compared with crochet threads, and that probably accounts for the fact that tatting always has been regarded as fragile. Washing instructions for tatting also treat it as very fragile, and we can only assume it was because of the fine thread and delicate work. This fine thread also made the manufacture of tatting a little slow and tedious, thereby discouraging its use on large pieces like tablecloths and bedspreads. A tatted shawl is known and large centerpieces have been seen.

150

Two styles and sizes of tatted edgings.

Each time the popularity of tatting soared—and that seems to have occurred about every fifteen to twenty years—new ideas in tatting began to appear. Directions and instructions found in the 1850s were limited to edgings. By 1885 the single-row tatted edgings had grown to widths of three or four inches, and there were instructions for making all-tatted doilies. Also new then were instructions for insertions and medallions that could be used on clothing as well as household linens.

In 1906 one article on tatting in *Home Needlework Magazine* began, "The gentle, old-fashioned art of tatting has come into its own again." It went on to say that the younger generation thought of tatting as an unknown quantity and believed it to consist of parts of garments that were yellowed with age and had been packed away in lavender and rose leaves. It is difficult to understand this statement since

tatting has been done continuously since it first began. There have been times when only a few tatters were working; at other times, around the turn of the century, for example, nearly everybody was tatting. It is still made today, and from all indications may be rounding the corner to another revival.

Reports abound of brides who insisted that most of their lingerie be made by the skilled needleworking nuns in Cuba and elsewhere. This same group insisted that not only their lingerie for the honeymoon but also that worn with the wedding dress be trimmed in tatted lace.

The layette for the new baby contained many examples of the tatter's art, including edgings for petticoats and dresses as well as tatted caps and medallions for both caps and coats. If the baby was a girl, she could expect to wear tatting on her clothing as long as she lived, on both underwear and outerwear.

![Tatted tea cart cover.](Tatted tea cart cover image)

Tatted tea cart cover.

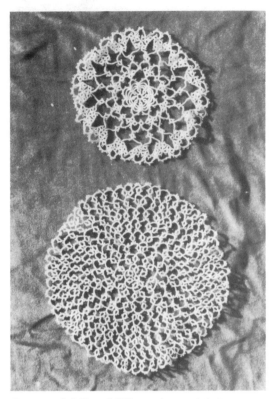

Two tatted doilies of different sizes and designs.

Shortly after the turn of the century, tatting began to be used in a number of new ways, including heavily starched (so they would stand alone) tatted nut bowls and baskets. No longer were the tatted edging on collars and cuffs enough—now the entire collar and cuffs were made entirely of tatting. About this time the jabot, a fancy, lacy frill that was fastened at the neck of a woman's dress or blouse, became popular. Some of the prettiest ones were made entirely of tatting. They are easy to recognize today as they were approximately eight to ten inches long, narrow at the top and flaring out six to seven inches at the bottom.

About this time fancy handbags or purses, often called "party bags," were made in tatting. The outside was tatted, the inside was lined with silks or satins, and it had ribbon draw-

Tatted baby cap with new ribbon rosettes.

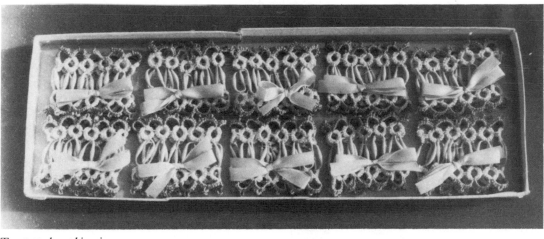

Ten tatted napkin rings.

Tatted yoke for camisole or corset cover.

strings. No longer were a couple of medallions sufficient for the baby's cap; now the entire cap had to be tatted. Ribbon was laced through the front and down the sides, and fancy rosettes were made for each side by tying a knot in a dozen or so lengths of ribbon and then fastened together at the base. Ribbon often was used with tatting as it complimented the lacy, open work. Yokes for nightgowns, chemises, and corset covers were also favorites of the tatters. Then they began making stacks of doilies and centerpieces in tatting. Napkin rings also were tatted.

Silk, linen, and cotton threads could be used in tatting, and tatting could be done with one or more shuttles. In fact, about this time it was becoming the accepted custom to tat with at least two shuttles; one just wasn't enough anymore.

As has been pointed out, each time the

Combination of crochet and tatting with tied linen thread fringe.

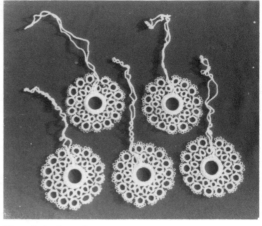

Tatted shade pulls.

popularity of tatting increased, new ideas and new pieces began to appear. About 1915, maybe earlier, the use of more than one color was introduced. Often a different shuttle was used for each color of thread, as it made the work easier. The popularity of this type of work lasted for a long time. Old towels often are found with red and white tatting made to match the white linen towels with red borders. Little girls' dresses from a later period have been seen with tatted edging on the white Peter Pan collars, the tatting done in two or more colors to match the colors in the fabric of the dress.

As late as 1923 instructions for tatted yokes for camisoles still were being given in some of the magazines. It was suggested that white batiste, fine and soft, was the best fabric to use with the dainty, tatted yokes. Another tatted item that was made earlier and continued to be popular into the 1920s was the boudoir cap.

As with all needlework, tatting was com-

bined with other types, but on a much smaller scale. Quite often it was seen on monogrammed towels and used to some extent with drawn work, but the majority was used with embroidery on embroidered doilies and centerpieces with tatted edging. A few instructions have been found for combining crocheting and tatting, but they are limited.

Antique tatting-related tools likely to be found today are the shuttles. The sterling silver examples are expensive (as is all sterling), but the late metal and celluloid ones are fairly plentiful and moderately priced. Lucky indeed is the collector who finds one of the old ring and pin or ring and chain tools used by the early tatters. They are much more likely to find the later gold hairpins that were used with eyeglasses.

Even easier to find are the tatted pieces, baby caps, yokes, centerpieces, doilies, and a few novelties like the tatted cross that was made for a bookmark. Also available are the centerpieces, doilies, towels, and tablecloths with tatted edging. It is difficult to find a stack of miscellaneous napkins that doesn't have at least a half dozen or so with tatted edgings.

CHAPTER 13

Knitting Through the Ages

To knit a stocking, needles four;
Cast on three needles and no more;
Each needle stitches eight and twenty,
Then one for the seam stitch will be plenty.

Those are the first four lines of a long knitting song entitled "A Stocking in Rhyme" that was popular in my great grandmother's day. It was even more popular in her grandmother's day, as that was the way all children and many adults learned to knit a few centuries ago. The song was necessary because there were few if any written instructions in those days. Like all other types of needlework, knitting was taught to very young children (age four or five), and these lessons were easier to teach while they chanted the knitting song. They sang as they worked, which kept them happy as they learned. It is thought this custom may have originated in England, as the knitting songs were so popular there.

Knitting has a long and colorful history, and some of it—like the legend of the ship from the Spanish Armada that was wrecked near Fair Isle—is even romantic. The sailors, after being rescued, settled down on the island and taught the natives how to knit. It is a well-known fact that early sailors practiced skilled and tedious arts and crafts during their long months at sea. Therefore, their knowledge of knitting was not unusual as they could have learned it in their own country or in some foreign port they had visited. At that time and for many years to come, men were as skilled as women in knitting.

Once the Fair Islanders had learned to knit, so the story goes, they passed the information on to people living in England and Scotland. The Scots always have claimed they invented or created knitting, and probably one of the reasons is the fact that the first knitting guild was named for one of their patron saints. This knitting guild was organized in Paris, but it took the name of St. Fiacre, one of the sons of a Scottish king. It is highly possible that knitting was first created in Scotland, as some ancient records have reports of Highlanders knitting warm clothing for the hard winters.

Then again, maybe this is not the case, as there are strong indications that knitting was known as early as the fifth century. It is known that in ancient times Arabs were excellent knitters, and made carpets and wall hangings. In those days people were searching eagerly for new ideas, and if they were given even a hint of how something was made in another country, they could usually make or build a reasonable facsimile. This very well could have been the way knitting was passed from one place to another. It may not have been knitting as we know it today, but it was similar.

We probably will never know where the Arabs learned knitting, but we do know that they were great traders. As they moved from one area to another, they could have picked up the basics of knitting and then passed it on as they traveled around selling their carpets and wall hangings. As each group learned, they could pass the information along to the next village and then on to the next all the way through Spain, Italy, Germany, France, and into England.

That supposition is also theory. No records were kept, so we can only surmise. Few if any of the early people could read and write, and they were much more interested in things other than the progress of knitting. For that reason it is impossible for us to know exactly when and where knitting actually originated and how it progressed. It is known from old records, however, that a different type of needle, one with a slight hook on the end similar to our present-day crochet hook, was used. This information has caused some controversy. Was this first work with the hooked needle actually crochet or was it knitting?

The word "knit" comes from the Anglo Saxon word *cnittan,* which means "threads woven by hand." It is believed that most of the early knitted items were articles of clothing. Knitting was developed into a highly skilled art by some of the better knitters, especially those with access to the finest yarns. One report mentions a shawl two yards square that was so fine and light that it could be passed through a wedding ring. Much of the credit for pieces like this would have to go to the spinners of the wool, for only the best in both wool and workmanship could produce yarn of that texture.

For the past century or so knitting has been considered women's work, although in the early days there were as many men as women knitting. In fact, there was a time when the entire family knitted. It was necessary to make enough warm clothing for the winter. Warm houses with plenty of insulation were unheard of, and the only heat in a home was furnished by fireplaces or cook stoves. Since fires were banked at night, extra bed covers and clothing were required.

Rather interesting is the fact that many shepherds knitted as they herded their sheep. That meant they were better qualified to know which breed of sheep produced the best wool or finest wool. In the 1800s it was said the finest wool came off the necks of the sheep. The

shepherds probably knew firsthand whether or not this was true. There are records of men knitting as they rode in their carts or wagons. They might be going to market or to visit, but they took their knitting along to do as they rode. No idle hands for these men. They also continued their knitting as they sat around the fire at night, and no doubt they joined the rest of the family in a knitting song.

Knitted stockings were one of the most important items made by early knitters. They were so important that itinerant stocking knitters traveled the countryside somewhat like the tinkers and menders, stopping along the way to help a mother catch up on her supply of winter stockings. They might make stockings for a family where no one was familiar with knitting. Professional stocking knitters were more skilled than the average knitter, so it was not unusual for them to be asked to make the silk stockings for dress wear for the entire family.

Those who think stockings, especially silk ones, weren't important at that time should read some of the reports that include information about a pair of fancy knitted silk stockings that were given to King Edward VI when he was a young man. The majority of the reports from England about knitting in the old days will include information about those silk stockings.

Stockings were so important that when the Englishman William Lee invented the stocking frame (a forerunner of the modern knitting machine), he received encouragement from neither his own countrymen nor the French when he later moved to France. The people feared that the machine would force stocking hand knitters out of work, and at that time knitting stockings by hand was big business.

Although silk, cotton, and wool yarn could be used in knitting, wool was the most popular because knitting in the early years was done primarily to make warm clothing. Gradually a change occurred in the hand-knitting industry as the newly invented knitting machines began to be used. They could make fabric and garments in a fraction of the time required to do it by hand. The machines had

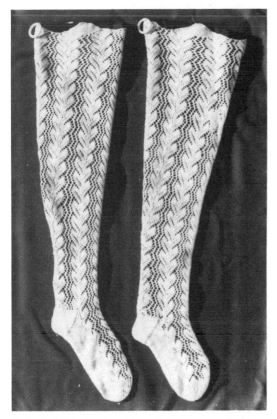

Pair of girl's knitted stockings. Ring was attached later so they could be hung for display.

---

little effect on some people, who continued to knit by hand. Probably the strongest reason was habit—their parents and grandparents had knitted their clothing, so why shouldn't they continue the practice? Money was another factor. They were accustomed to shearing the sheep, cleaning and dyeing the wool, spinning the yarn, and knitting the garments—and it didn't cost them a penny. But to go to the store and buy the ready-made garments cost more than some poor people could afford. For that reason alone they continued to knit.

Slowly the men stopped knitting. In fact, there was a general yet gradual decline in the amount of hand knitting being done.

By 1850 there was no mention of men knitting, but it was suggested that people with poor eyesight, the aged, and the invalid could find much pleasure in knitting. Knitting could

be a "toil" or a pleasure, they said, it all depended on whether or not one learned to hold their hands correctly while knitting. Like all other needlework, knitting depended on the thread or yarn to make the design, the decoration, and the item itself. The tools or needles were so simple they were almost primitive.

In knitting one could use either two, four, or sometimes five needles. The old needles were made of steel, ivory, bone, or wood. They came in varying degrees of fineness or thickness and in lengths that varied from around ten to twenty inches. The older needles were longer than those made around the turn of this century.

In all the early instructions, the emphasis was on learning the correct way to do the work in the beginning. All the early instructions not only gave directions for making various stitches and items of clothing and household linens, but they also explained in detail the correct way to do it.

An example of that found in some 1858 instructions stressed the importance of the "position of the hands" when knitting. The right-hand needle should be laid over the hand, they said, between the thumb and forefinger, and one should train the thumb to stay close to the needle and not move with every stitch. The page-long dissertation on hand positions ended with the information that the forefinger of the left hand, "with its delicate and sensitive tip," should be used to check each stitch and push it up to the point of the needle. "By coming to an understanding with this most useful member," Mrs. Pullan wrote, "you will soon find that it will keep you perfectly informed of the nature of the stitch next to be knitted, and its susceptibility may be cultivated until you can perform the most delicate work as well in the dark as in the light."

Knitting was never as popular for household linens as the other types of needlework, but around 1890 numerous instructions began to appear for making various types of knitted lace or edgings. It was recommended for use on pillowcases, towels, doilies, and centerpieces. It was not widely used on clothing, except on a few pieces like petticoats, chemises, and corset covers that would have a row here and there. Some doilies and centerpieces were completely knitted, but crocheted pieces probably outnumbered them a thousand to one. Judging by the number of pieces found today, either in solid knitting or with knitted edging, it would seem safe to say that knitting on household linens was somewhere near the bottom of the popularity scale.

Regardless of its popularity, knitting continued to be done. In fact, there has never been a time when it wasn't done to some extent, although the majority of items made were knitted wool sweaters, shawls, stockings, and other heavy winter garments. Many knitted bedspreads were made.

During the last decade of the 1800s, there was hardly a needlework publication that didn't include instructions for knitting stockings or boots. In northern areas knitted stockings were almost essential.

Although knitting wasn't often combined with crochet, it was used with embroidery—especially on embroidered towels, doilies and centerpieces. Monogrammed towels often were finished off with knitted lace or edging. Pillowcases with drawn work and knitted edging have been seen, but apparently they were not too plentiful.

Knitting never seemed to experience revivals like other types of needlework. Then, around the turn of the century, knitting suffered another blow. A small knitting machine was developed that could be bought and used at home. In 1890 they were being advertised as "family knitters" that could "knit everything required for the household of any quality, texture, and weight desired." The women continued to hand-knit special garments, but for the everyday items they used the small knitting machine if they could afford one. If the maker became really skilled on the machine, the items looked almost handmade. The machine produced items much faster than hand knitting. While it might take months to make an item by

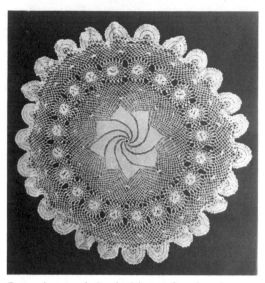

Centerpiece was knitted with very fine thread.

hand, it could be made on the machine in a week or less.

Surprisingly, there are more hand knitters today than at any time since before the turn of the century. In some areas they have formed guilds and have public sales once or twice a year.

One thing that seemed to trigger renewed interest in knitting a decade or so ago was the desire for beautiful sweaters to wear on the ski slopes. Knitting has been done through the years, even if on a limited basis, but during the past decade or so its popularity seems to have skyrocketed. Some knitters are even raising their own sheep so they can control the quality of the yarn.

Knitting, like other needlework, was made with a simple needle (knitting needle) and some thread or yarn, so there are no antique tools related to this work except the needles. Old needles are extremely scarce, and so are the old knitted household linens. There is little or no demand for old knitted clothing.

CHAPTER 14
The Family of Lace

Volumes could be written about old lace—and many have been—but none cover the lace story completely. It would be almost impossible to find and combine all the information, including the legends, in any book. Although many types of needlework resulted in edgings, insertions, and small articles called lace, only two types—needlepoint (often called needle lace) and bobbin (or pillow lace)—actually qualify for the title of genuine handmade lace.

To really learn how lace was made, how to separate the handmade from the machine-made lace, and how to recognize a particular type of lace at a glance would require years of study and comparison. To become an expert on lace, one would have to visit museums where all types of old handmade lace were displayed, study them, and then compare them with machine-made lace of the same type and period. It is not likely the average collector will

Lace pillow with an assortment of bobbins.

find many examples of the really old lace outside museums and private collections. Unless one is planning to become a connoisseur or pay high prices for lace, just learning which is old and which type one prefers is sufficient.

One of the older books on lace that would be extremely helpful to anyone beginning a study of lace, provided it can be found, is *The Lace Book* by Jessie F. Caplin, published in 1932. This book is especially helpful in identifying the different types of lace, as there are many illustrations, descriptions, and notes on comparison.

For a study of lacemaking and its revival or survival in Belgium before and after World War I, Charlotte Kellog's *Bobbins of Belgium,* published in 1920, is recommended. Although the basis of the book is primarily concerned with the progress of lacemaking and the people who sponsored and created organizations to preserve and protect lacemaking, the twenty-five page Appendix is strictly technical in that it has drawings of various stitches and patterns and identifies various types of bobbins.

For simple identification and instructions, the most helpful book would probably be a *A Lace Guide for Makers and Collectors* by Gertrude Whiting, published in 1920. There is a section on explanation and nomenclature plus approximately two hundred pages of rules for making lace. Each page contains a photo and instructions. In a pocket in the back is a large diagram described as "An Indexed, Comparative Sampler of 145 Bobbin Lace Grounds and Fillings." Twenty-eight different types of bobbins are shown and labeled.

Although these books are old, they are not impossible to find. Copies quite often are offered by old book dealers, and most large libraries have books like this at least in the reference department.

When we said that volumes had been written on the subject of lace, it was not an exaggeration. In the bibliography of her book, Whiting lists nearly two thousand sources. Of course many of these are only articles found in various magazines, but it shows how extensively the lace story has been covered throughout the years.

Perhaps it is the light, airy texture of lace that brings out the poet in every writer who has ever written on the subject. They always refer to it in glowing terms like "gossamer webs," "a fairy fabric," and the "flowering and fragility" of lace. Contrary to its fragile appearance, lace is quite strong, durable, and substantial. It had to be to be used in so many ways on milady's clothing. It was used on her lingerie and negligees whether they were made of dainty muslin, rich velvet, shiny satin, or costly brocades. Lace was used on scarves, mantles (a loose sleeveless garment similar to our present-day lady's vest), fans, parasols, and head- and footwear. Lace also was used on dresses, blouses, coats, petticoats, and pantlets.

When lace was in its infancy, it was so expensive that only the very wealthy could afford to wear it. Even then kings who were jealous that excessive use might render it common issued decrees and proclamations forbidding anyone that did not have a titled prefix on his name from wearing it.

There are numerous legends concerning the wearing of lace and the ordinances against it. Some, like the 1299 A.D. ruling that regulated the wearing apparel of people of all ages and made special mention of the use of lace on clothing, could have confused lace with other types of needlework. Since most researchers agree that lace originated around the sixteenth century (a few still say the eleventh century), this substantiates the belief of many that old references to lace found in many ancient manuscripts and records was actually confused with embroidery. This would be easy to do because embroidery is the oldest type of needlework and was done in some very lacy, intricate designs. In fact, it was the intricacy of cutwork that was said to have been the inspiration for the first needle lace. Some of the cutwork and some of the drawn work was so lavishly done on the fabric that it would have been easy for someone unfamiliar with needlework to call it lace. It also must be remembered that Chaldean, Hebrew, and Arabic languages did not differentiate between the two in those early writings.

But the legends or the ruling and ordinances are interesting, nevertheless—

especially the one that decreed no woman whose station in life was less than that of a knight's wife "could deck herself out with lace or passement lace in gold or silver" during the reign of Queen Mary of England. She also was prohibited from wearing sleeves, partlet (a covering for the neck and chest that often was ruffled and embroidered), or linens trimmed with "purls" of gold and silver, whitework, or cutwork made byond the seas. This was not done so much to cut down on imports, they said, as it was to protect the English lacemakers. The theory was that if foreign laces were not brought in, the supply would remain low and thereby cause prices to stay high. What this decree did was increase smuggling. But limiting the number of persons who can use or wear a certain thing like lace has never been the answer to pricing. Supply and demand always has controlled prices.

Apparently most of these rules or decrees were repealed or ignored, as it is a well-known fact that nobody in his court was better dressed than Henry VIII. He and the rest of the citizenry who could afford it bedecked themselves in all types of laces, both locally made and imported. Reports on the hedonistic king always mention his fancy clothing, including all the needlework and handkerchiefs that were described as "fringed with gold." Queen Elizabeth loved fancy needlework on her clothing, and it was said that her petticoats for court or social affairs "fairly bristled with gold lace." Around the house or castle, she wore petticoats with silver lace.

In Queen Elizabeth's time being overdressed in the finest of needlework and laces was considered chic. Portraits of many of the rulers and some of the wealthy private citizens of that time attest to the fact.

Although France, Spain, and Flanders have all claimed credit for creating bobbin or pillow lace, historians almost unanimously have agreed that recognition belongs to the Italian nuns. It is known that the majority of all needlework in the early days was done by nuns in the various convents. Since communication in those days was nearly nonexistent, it would be impossible to say without fear of contradiction who first created lace. It is quite possible that the nuns in several convents were working on the same idea at the same time, but due to the lack of communication, it was years before anyone had a chance to compare work or try to time it correctly for credit purposes. Those dedicated nuns were not trying to make history or be given credit for creating something new. Their only purpose was to create something beautiful for the church vestments and linens.

Everyone accepts the fact that lace was created by the nuns. Nevertheless, there is one widely circulated legend about the origin of lace that is quite romantic. It is the story of the young girl who made a fishnet for the young fisherman to whom she was betrothed. The young man only used the net once before he went into the service in his country's navy, and the only things he caught in the net that time were some grass and rocks. Knowing he could be gone for a long time, the young fisherman left his net with his bride-to-be. She was depressed over their separation and wept bitterly. As she wept she clung to the fishnet, the one link between her and her lover. As she wept and clung to the net, she wound the delicate strands in and out of the net, then she twisted the threads as she threw the weights, using them as the later lacemakers used the bobbins. When she finally dried her eyes enough to see the fishnet, she realized she had created something so beautiful it was almost beyond belief. She overcame her grief and continued to work with threads, so the story goes, until she was producing the finest of pillow lace.

The term lace is often added to work like crochet, tatting, or hairpin, but there are only two kinds of genuine handmade lace. They are the pillow or bobbin lace and needlepoint. As the name implies, pillow lace is made on a pillow held in the worker's lap. A design or pattern is drawn or pricked on paper (usually colored paper so the worker knows where to put her pins as the work progresses). The thread is wound on the bobbins that are hung over the pattern so they can be worked in pairs, as pillow lace is a form of weaving.

Each pair of bobbins is used to weave through the warp from side to side, and is passed through only two warp threads on each throw. When making lace edgings or insertions (and records show that the very first laces made were actually insertions), the paper pattern is put on the revolving cylinder so the pattern can be repeated as many times as necessary producing unlimited amounts of lace insertion or edging.

When the lacemaker only wanted small figures or flowers, a small spray of flowers, scrolls, or medallions, each was made on a small round cushion or pillow and then worked into the design. There are several ways of incorporating these small pieces into the overall design. One way was to simply whip or with fine stitches sew them onto a net background, or they could be included into the overall design by working the background around them and then fastening them using either a needle or with the bobbins.

Lace teachers through the ages always have believed that Torchon lace was the easiest to make and therefore best suited for teaching beginners. But before any lessons began the students were carefully instructed in all phases of the work, beginning with the correct use of the pillow. It had to be the correct size so that when it was placed in the lap it would be at a convenient height for both the hands and the eyes. Lacemaking was and is extremely hard on the maker's eyes because she has to watch so many threads so carefully. The exception, of course, was a worker who made the same pattern repeatedly, like the edgings and insertions that were made for sale to the masses. She soon became so accustomed to the pattern that she could almost do it with her eyes closed, especially if she was working with heavy thread.

The next step was selecting the correct bobbins. They came in a variety of sizes to fit the type and size of thread to be used. Lace could be made using gold, silver, linen, silk, or cotton threads in sizes that ranged from heavy to spiderweb fine. Pins also were selected on that basis; large, heavy pins were used for the coarse lace made of pure linen thread and smaller pins were used for the silks and fine English threads.

Once the student had selected the correct pins, patterns, thread, and bobbins, the next step was to work toward becoming adept at manipulating the bobbins, which was no easy task for a beginner. Before the actual practice began, there was one more thing to learn. They must become familiar with the terms used in pillow lacemaking. Fortunately, there were only two: the whole throw and the half throw. Until the worker could become familiar with them, both sounded unbelievably intricate. Actually they were not too difficult—with a little practice anyone could become an expert in either or both.

The whole throw was and is made by taking a pair of bobbins in the left hand and another in the right hand. Regardless of which bobbin comes into each hand, those in the left will be known as No. 1 and No. 2 while those in the right hand will be No. 3 and No. 4. The first movement is to pass the No. 2 bobbin over the No. 3 bobbin into the right hand, and then take No. 3 in the left hand. The second movement requires that the No. 4 bobbin be passed over No. 3 and at the same time pass No. 2 over No. 1. This movement, according to experts, can best be done by inserting the forefinger of the right hand with the palm up between threads No. 3 and No. 4. Then, with a movement of the wrist, turn the palm down and twist No. 4 over No. 3. Working the threads in the left hand is a bit different, as the forefingers must be inserted between No. 1 and No. 2 threads in such a way that the back of the hand rather than the palm will be up. Then as the palm is turned up, No. 2 thread will be twisted over No. 1.

To make the half throw, execute the first and second movement of the whole throw, but repeat it until it can be done mechanically, efficiently, and rapidly.

Now that the lace student had mastered the throws, she was ready to practice making lace on the pillow. Two parallel rows of holes were pricked in a colored card or in stiff paper. This was pinned to the pillow so the holes ran up and down or around the cylinder. Seven pairs of bobbins were fastened directly above the cylinder. The worker was ready to practice simple Torchon lace stitches. A whole throw was made with the first and second pair of bobbins. Then, holding the first pair of bobbins between the thumb and forefinger of the left hand, the second pair was passed between the third and fourth fingers of that hand keeping the threads straight. The worker then took a pin in the right hand and passed it between the pairs just above the fingers of the left hand and pushed it up and into the first hole on the left, still keeping the pairs of bobbin threads separate. She closed in the pin with a whole throw.

Laying aside the first pair, she took the second pair in the left hand and made a whole throw with the third pair and in sequence made a whole throw with each of the seven pairs of bobbins. Holding the sixth and seventh pairs, she puts a pin between them and into the first hole on the right. She closes in the pin with a whole throw, lays the seventh pair aside, and works back through the pairs of bobbins, making whole throws with each pair in turn. The next pin was placed on the left side and the side-to-side weaving continued. When the student became proficient in whole throws, she could practice half throws the same way.

Needlepoint or needle lace, on the other hand, was made with only a needle and thread. One of the reasons there is more interest today in bobbin or pillow lace is the fact that people can better understand how it was made and they have tools with which to work. Actually, bobbin or pillow lace was easier to make, less tedious, and always has had more followers. It also was much easier to adapt to machine making; it was a long time before a machine was developed that would produce needlepoint lace.

All that was necessary to make needlepoint lace by hand was a needle, thread, and infinite patience. Some argue that needle lace was the outgrowth of cutwork while others insist that it originated from a type of hemstitching similar to Italian hemstitching (where only one thread was pulled for each row of holes necessary to make the design). Then they improved on that design by making several rows of hemstitching on a thread or two away from the one before it. The worker then began drawing several threads in one place (rather than the single thread they formerly had pulled). The next step was to make shorter pulls, cut the thread away, and fill the opening with designs and bars made of new thread. As the designs grew in number, it was necessary to reinforce the work with stitches like buttonhole stitches. During the sixteenth century the cloth background was eliminated or discarded, and the lace was made entirely on a groundwork of thread. Needlepoint lace was born.

Contrary to legends and some disagreements, most people also give credit for the creation of needlepoint lace to the nuns in the Italian convents. That is the logical solution, as they were not only skilled needleworkers, but they also constantly were striving to make finer, better, and more beautiful things for the church.

As the so-called secrets of lacemaking spread (the people outside the convents learned to make it), it became more plentiful. As the supply of pieces grew, more people were able to wear and use it. The average man on the street was not allowed to wear lace until the eighteenth century, but the wealthy and the titled nobility could use or wear as much as they could afford. But the day was coming when everybody—prince and peasant alike—could swathe themselves in lace-trimmed clothing from head to foot, even if some of it was machine made.

The world was on that slow road to the machine age. The trend toward machine-made lace was a long process. It actually started around 1589, when William Lee invented his unpopular stocking frame. But it didn't become a reality for bobbin lace until around 1807, when John Heathcoat invented his first bobbin net machine. In the interim there had been a little "net" made on variations of the stocking frame in 1760, but it was more or less a stocking without the regular shape. It was described as irregular, imperfect, and heavy, but it was bought by the poorer people who were starved for lace of any type to use on their clothing. They wanted to copy what they had seen on the famous and the mighty.

All the time ingenious men were striving to invent a machine that would make beautiful, artistic lace that would be almost as pretty as the handmade version yet so much faster and easier to make. Around 1769 a man named

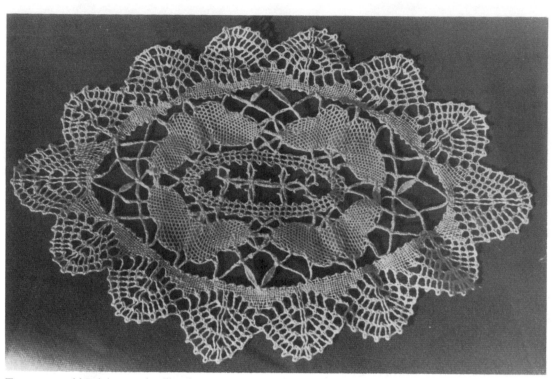

Twenty-year-old Belgian-made pillow lace.

Robert Frost finally produced a lightweight net on a variation of the stocking frame and then embroidered tiny, simple flowers on it by hand. This device was no threat to the handmade lacemakers, but progress was being made toward the development of a lacemaking machine.

Then in 1807 John Heathcoat of Derby, England, invented the first bobbin net machine. This machine was completely different from the stocking machine, a break that was essential if lace ever was to be made by machine. Inventors had long tried to vary the stocking frame, thinking that was the way to create a lacemaking machine. Heathcoat proved them wrong. Writers and merchants predicted the end of handmade lace, and a great rivalry began although little ever came of it. Those who could afford the handmade laces continued to use them on outside clothing while undergarments and boudoir pieces might have machine-made lace.

In later years John Heathcoat and Company moved to Fifth Avenue in New York City, and it was there that the company published a small booklet telling of Heathcoat's life and his inventions. It said in part that while he was a young man growing up near Derby, he was, like other young men of that period, apprenticed to a warp frame builder. It was this training, no doubt, that gave him the background necessary for building the lace machine. The booklet writer described him as "displaying unusual intelligence and mechanical ability," and by the time he was twenty-one years old he was in business for himself as a repairer and installer of warp frames. Apparently they were correct, as by this time he had patented several small mechanical improvements in the frames.

His first bobbin net machine was a great improvement over the stocking frame variations the others had created, but it was far from perfect. He was constantly working on improvements on this machine, and in 1809 he patented one that was so much better it sold by the hundreds in both England and France.

Heathcoat is credited with inventing the

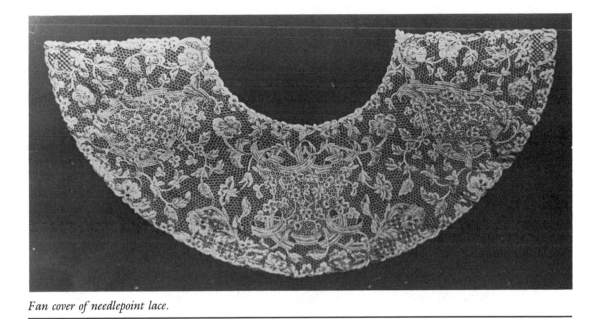
Fan cover of needlepoint lace.

first lacemaking machine, but it was John Levers who in 1813 invented a machine able to make lace as wide as eighteen inches. It has been described as a great improvement over the Heathcoat machines as it would make figured lace more easily. Then in 1834 an English mechanic name Draper converted the Lever machine to the Jacquard. The Jacquard system recently had been invented in France to be used on cloth or fabric looms. This movement controlled the warp threads so the pattern could be repeated over the length of the fabric. After Mr. Draper's conversion the pattern in lace could be repeated automatically across the width of the machine, which was 230 inches. This allowed many narrow strips of lace to be made at one time and had a drastic effect on prices. Now pretty machine-made lace that was almost impossible to differentiate from handmade lace could be made and sold at prices the masses could afford.

Man had finally mastered the technique of bobbin or pillow lace on a machine, but needlepoint continued to defy the skills of the most ingenious inventors. But the day finally came when a machine was invented that could produce beautiful needlepoint lace. Like everything where the exact history is not known, there are legends. One of the legends concern-

ing the discovery of ways to make needlepoint lace by machine centers around a French factory worker. One day the worker accidentally dropped a piece of silk chiffon embroidered in fine cotton into a tub filled with an alkaline solution. He was horrified when he fished the fabric out to find that it simply fell apart. But as he looked closer, he discovered that the animal section (silk base) was, indeed, gone, but the vegetable (cotton) embroidery was intact.

Whether this was an average worker or one of the mechanical geniuses of that era is unknown, but according to legend the man realized the importance of his discovery and immediately went to work on ways to utilize it. In short order, he found a way to make needlepoint lace by machine.

A century ago silk needlepoint lace was made by first steeping thin cotton muslin in a solution of sulfuric acid. This process did not prevent the pattern from being embroidered on the fabric. When the work was completed, the entire piece was placed in a highly heated stove where the cotton was consumed and the silk remained intact. This is the complete reversal of the way the legend describes the theory, but then legends have a way of getting turned around.

At one time there were 150 thousand

Fine, machine-made lace was used mostly on children's clothes and lingerie.

women earning a living making lace in Belgium. France claimed twice that number, while Spain, Germany, and England claimed a large portion of the women in their countries depended on lacemaking for a living. The lacemaking machines had a terrific effect on the lacemakers. Suddenly they had to face the fact that they could be forced out of work by machines that could do the same thing they were doing in a fraction of the time and at a fraction of the cost. Fortunately, many were able to continue to make their lace—not as many as before—but enough to supply the demands for genuine handmade lace. Conditions were not nearly as bad as had been forecast, because about the time the machines became a reality, the American markets were thrown open to trade. People with money continued to buy the more expensive handmade lace to which they had become accustomed, and the lacemakers continued to ply their needles.

The word "lace" did not come into universal use until the beginning of the eighteenth century. It came from two words, *lacinia* meaning "hem or fringe of a garment," and *lacez*, a braid. Lacemakers in the early years were called *passementiers*. Until this century,

the most universal term for lace was *passement au fuseau* for bobbin or pillow lace and *passement a l'aiguille* for needlepoint. From these two types of lace have come a wide variety of laces, each with its own name and character.

Today there are so many machine-made laces that are perfect replicas of the handmade laces that it is difficult for anyone who has not made a thorough study of lace to sort one from the other. The average antique dealer or auctioneer doesn't have the time to study laces. There isn't that much money to be made from them, so they are sold "as is." This leaves the burden of classification on the collector, if she is that interested. The majority of people buy old lace because it appeals to them or they have a use for it. Until recently most of the boxes of old lace found at estate sales or auctions were bought by doll collectors to be used to make clothing for their dolls. After all, the old-fashioned dolls were much better dressed in their day than the average person.

Now the tables have turned and prices on old lace are skyrocketing. The main reason for this is the fact that old lace is being "recycled"—used to trim or decorate some of the more expensive dresses and blouses in exclu-

Coarsely made laces were used more on household linens.

Lace collar.

sive dress shops. This trend has not gone unnoticed by those who make their own clothes. A recent news story pointed out the excessive use of new lace by this year's French designers. Another news story told of a New York designer who is making expensive one-of-a-kind dresses trimmed with old lace she has found at rummage sales, estate auctions, and in antique shops.

The past few years have seen a revival of lace, not only in use but in the return to making handmade laces. Women are now searching for lace pillows to use in lacemaking, not as decorative objects. Many of these new lacemakers have banded together in a far-flung association that is kept close by regular bulletins and newsletters. Most of the information in the newsletters is about new finds in the lace field and instructions on lacemaking.

Without extensive study few people will ever know the different types of old lace; all they will know is that this piece is prettier than that one. It is only when they get into deep study that they will learn that names for the same type of lace varied from one place to another and the background design which usually denotes a specific type has been changed through the years. Even though a collector really has no desire to delve into lacemaking and its history, she still should know the names of the most popular types.

During the Victorian era ribbon was used profusely, therefore laces were made with places for the ribbon to be laced through.

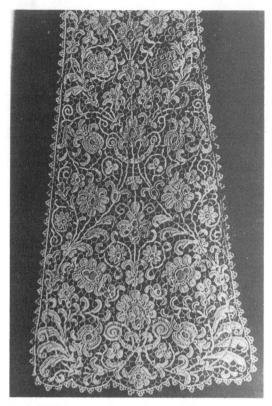

Early Irish lace panel.

Alençon, a needlepoint lace, is associated with weddings, and has been called one of the glories of France. Manufacture began around 1665 in the town of Alençon. For a century or more all of it was made within a few miles of the town, yet it furnished employment for around nine thousand lacemakers. Kings and emperors played a part in the history of Alençon lace. In France as elsewhere during wars and revolutions, nonessentials like lacemaking were forgotten, but Napoleon must be given credit for bringing the Alençon lacemakers as well as other French lacemakers back to work. He did it with orders for such things as a layette for the newborn son of the king of Italy and bed hangings for Marie Louise.

This was just an extension of its greatness, as Alençon had reached its full glory under the reigns of Louis XIV and Louis XV. Louis XIV established a school for lacemakers so they could be trained correctly. He then opened trade routes with other countries so the lace could be sold all over the world. The heights of popularity that Alençon lace reached during the reigns of the two kings was fantastic. Everyone who could afford it used lace on every piece of wearing apparel as well as in their boudoirs. Floor to ceiling bed hangings were made of Alençon lace, as were covers or hangings to hide their baths. Smaller pieces were made to drape their toilette (what we would now call a vanity). With such widespread and varied uses, one might get the mistaken idea that Alençon lace was not expensive, but the bill for bed hangings for the Duke of York amounted to approximately $4,000—a tidy sum for lace bed hangings even in the eighteenth century.

With the coming of the machine age, Alençon lace lost much of its original popularity—it was one of the first of the needlepoints to be made by machine. Alençon lace made on the machine was so well received that lacemakers discontinued the line except on special order from old and wealthy customers who were willing to pay the price for the "real" thing.

The machine-made versions of *Argentan* and Alençon are so similar that it is difficult for the advanced collector to distinguish between them. If one could find enough of the old handmade examples to do an extensive study, it might be easier to place them in the right category. Before the advent of machine-made Argentan, old lacemakers spent months and years creating pieces of this lovely old needlepoint lace. It was made of fine linen thread, and the open mesh ground was worked in fine buttonhole stitches. Argentan, named for the town where it was made, is one of only two needle laces attributed to France, and counted among its many customers was Madame du Barry. Like so many of the other handmade laces, Argentan is no longer available—except perhaps on special order for some royal family.

When the production of a specific type of lace was confined to one small area and the work was taught and controlled by the old lacemakers, it usually was difficult to tell one worker's lace from another. But when it began to be made in other areas there were variations. When the manufacture moved to another country, the variations were even more noticeable, and this compounds the work of the lace collector today.

This is not a new problem as attention was called to this fact in 1920 in an article appearing in *Needlecraft Magazine*. The first paragraph pinpoints the condition. "Few old world laces now retain their distinctive character. Alençon, formerly made only in France, is now turned out by the yard in Venice. Rose point, a name once applied only to Flemish laces, is made in Italy as well as Belgium while Irish crocheted laces are as common in New York lace factories as in Dublin."

The article went on to say that the only exception to that rule was Armenian lace, made by women of the Near East. Most of the Armenian lace offered for sale in America was imported because the Armenian women and girls living here kept most of the lace they made. They had little interest in the commercial value and kept it because of the artistry involved. This is interesting for two reasons. One, we know that as late as 1920 there still was some needle lace being made—and it was being made in America. This brings us to the second reason: The lace is available today.

Apparently the Armenians were as dedicated to their lacemaking as the people of other countries, as little girls were taught from infancy to make the beautiful needle laces. This included all girls—those from peasant, middle- and upper-class families. They were taught to make and appreciate the exquisite needle laces, a trait they brought with them when they came to America. But it would be safe to say that the lace they made after their arrival differed somewhat from that made in the old country. If nothing else, they had to use a different type of thread.

Binche was another lace where it is almost impossible for even the advanced collector to sort the handmade from the machine made. This type also was made on the circular machine, where the threads were worked in the same way as those twisted by hand. Binche only can be made in one width at a time, making it relatively expensive even in the machine-made version. Like so many of the bobbin or pillow laces, Binche was given the name of the town in Belgium where it originated.

Bruges is another well-known pillow or bobbin lace that is still being made by hand in Belgium, where it was created. Bruges is a very impressive lace, and although it is a bit coarser than Duchesse, it is quite similar in both design and appearance. It is a very desirable type of lace and was and still is made in small doilies as well as edgings and insertions.

In the beginning *Brussels* lace was made both on the pillow and as needlepoint. The pillow laces were made for those unable to afford the more expensive needle laces. The fine needle lace was one of the exquisite French laces that was smuggled into England when there were so many ordinances against anyone other than royalty wearing lace. The finest of this lace was made with handspun linen thread, a custom that still prevails when lace is to be made for a royal wedding. The background net, often called bobbin net or bobbinet, was the first lace of sorts to be made on the Heathcoat machine in 1808. Once it could be machine made, the next step was machine embroidery. The machine net and lace were made in several degrees of fineness and coarseness. The bobbinet was used for everything from curtains to the background of wedding dresses decorated with decor crochet.

Chantilly lace is probably the best known of all bobbin or pillow laces because it was and still is so popular for wedding veils. It originated around 1740 in the town of Chantilly, France. Originally it was made of raw silk of a soft ecru color (called blonde) and in black. In fact, Chantilly always has been famous for its black laces, and in later years it was known for the white. Marie Antoinette was very fond of this lace and used it by the yard. During the revolution the lace workers who did not go into hiding were beheaded because it was felt they had contributed to the extravagances of the nobility. But by 1805 the lacemakers were back at work. When the lace-making machine was first developed, Chantilly lace was one of the most popular types made, and that popularity continues today. Chantilly lace has been made with silk, linen, and cotton threads.

Another of the better-known laces was *Cluny*, a pillow lace with a long history that some say dates back to the fifteenth century. Cluny originally was a form of netting with the design or pattern worked on it with counted stitches like darning. In the early days the stitchery was done in gold, silver, or some heavy type of thread, but later a shiny thread was used to make the design more outstanding. As all types of laces became more popular and prices more competitive, lacemakers switched to linen thread. Cluny lace became plentiful soon after the missionaries began teaching the Chinese how to make it. At one time there were more Chinese than Europeans engaged in lacemaking, and they began sending large amounts of Cluny lace to both America and Europe. They used cotton thread, which made their lace much less expensive than that made in Europe. When machine-made Cluny hit the market, it meant the end of this type of handmade lace.

Duchesse is another pillow lace that was and still is used frequently for weddings and has been reproduced in carload lots on the machine. It was made with a finer thread than most, but it had a larger and bolder design. Flowers and leaves are the designs most commonly used on Duchesse, with the primrose being the favorite.

Filet was the plainest of all laces. It was also the least expensive, but it was a durable little lace usually made in narrow edgings. Filet began as net and was fashioned after the nets used by fishermen. Once the background was completed, a pattern of sorts was worked on the net and the edges were done in a buttonhole stitch to help strengthen it. Filet was both handmade by the Chinese and machine made, neither of which helped to increase its desirability. Antique filet lace was made by using a braidlike design or pattern loosely fastened to the basic net. In some cases this was combined with a touch of needlework to fill in the net. To make Tuscan filet extra thread or threads were worked in an embroidery or scrolllike design on the net.

Mechlin (also called *Malins*) lace actually didn't reach its peak of popularity until well into the eighteenth century. At that time it was considered the only lace for ruffles, cravats, and other furbelows. Of course, with people like Queen Charlotte expressing a preference for it, how could it lose? With popularity came extensive demands, and high prices followed close behind. It was one of the most expensive of the Belgium pillow laces. It was so sheer and beautiful that it often was called "summer lace," while the heavier Alençon was called "winter lace." Because it was so pretty and was not too expensive, the machine-made Mechlin became very popular and was used for nearly a century as edgings for handkerchiefs and for trimming lingerie.

Point de Paris was a bobbin or pillow lace that later was copied on the circular machine, where the movement of the threads duplicated those used in making pillow lace. That makes it extremely difficult to distinguish the handmade from the machine-made versions today—and if this is confusing for experts, it would be next to impossible for the average collector to differentiate between the two. Much of this lace was made in edgings and insertions and was used on lingerie and household linens.

Rose point (also called *point* lace) was one of those exquisite needle laces that was used extensively for wedding dresses and accessories. Both the Italians and the Spanish claim credit for the invention of rose point, and probably no one will ever know for sure when or if the lace originated in either country. It is possible that as the church transferred nuns from one convent to another, they could have taken new ideas they were working on and completed them at the new location. The ones left at the former convent naturally would claim credit because they knew the work began there, and the ones at the new location would feel that since it was developed at their place, credit belonged to them. Rose point is fine and dainty—perfect for wedding finery—with a delicate net background on which elaborate designs have been worked. Even in later years the machine-made Rose point was still fine, dainty, and very desirable. Due to the interest of the Belgian people and the work of the lace committees, all types of lace, including rose point, were made longer in that country than in any other.

Torchon was so simple to make that lace instructors usually began with it when teaching new students. Once students learned to make it, they sometimes continued to make it rather than learn something new. Not all lace students followed that route; many just used the simplicity of Torchon as a learning tool, and as soon as they had mastered this easy step they went on to the more intricate types. Since Torchon was so easy to learn, it was taught in all the countries where the missionaries were trying to teach new skills and trades. It is one of the best known of all laces, and at one time it was called beggars' lace for reasons unknown. Made with both linen and cotton threads, the machine-made Torchon was plentiful and cheap.

Valenciennes is a beautiful pillow lace that was named for the Belgian town where it originated. Later the town was transferred to France under a treaty arrangement. This was probably one of the best things that could have happened to the town and the lace it manufactured, because it was during this time that Louis XIV took a special interest in lacemaking in general. The business became so large that at one time there were over fourteen thousand people in the town of Valenciennes alone employed in lacemaking. With so many people involved in making lace, it would seem that there would be an abundance, but it must be remembered that it might take one worker a year or even two years to complete the hangings for one bed or the wedding veil for one princess because the work was so intricate.

This is another example of the in-depth study one would have to do to become a connoisseur of lace. At one time, over a century ago, there were six centers—Yres, Alost, Bruges, Courtrai, Ghent, and Menin—where Valenciennes lace was made. That alone would not pose a problem. The problem arises from the fact that each center used an identifying mark so their work could be recognized anywhere. Now it is only a matter of finding which mark was used at each center. Then there was one other known discrepancy: each used a slightly different ground. In some it was the twisting of the bobbins—two-and-one-half times at Ghent and five times at Alost.

Belgium often has been called the "Lacemaking country" as it was there that Queen Elizabeth not only sought ways to improve conditions for lacemakers, but also gave encouragement so they would continue their work. As late as 1911 a group of prominent Belgian women (with royal approval from the queen) organized the Friends of Lace. The aim of this group was to improve teaching techniques, shorten work hours (many lacemakers labored over their pillows for as long as fourteen hours a day), and increase the low wages. The latter was an incentive to get young people—who were taking other jobs where the wages were better, the hours shorter, and the work less tedious—to attend lace school. The organization began to subsidize the establishment of lace schools where the student was not only taught to make lace, but also was given enough education to enable her to make her own designs. With the beginning of World War I, the first thoughts of the Friends of Lace were how to better care for the lace workers, as it was common knowledge that during any conflict the lace workers were the first to lose their incomes. It didn't happen this time thanks to a large grant from the United States that enabled the Friends of Lace to immediately form the Brussels Lace Committee.

Pillow or bobbin lace can be made with as few as a dozen different threads or with as many as several hundred. It was said that three hundred bobbins were required to make Valenciennes lace in two-inch widths, and it was not uncommon in those early days to see a worker using as many as twelve hundred bobbins when working on the intricate lace hangings, but needle lace was made with one technique—a needle and thread. The skill of the lacemaker determined the variety of stitches used in needle lace. A beginner often only used one stitch while the more experienced worker might use as many as one hundred different stitches (or "points" as they were called).

Other laces were known by other names in other places, but this is an example of the magnitude of the lacemaking industry in its prime. Today there is a trend back to making lace by hand. Although it is tedious and time-consuming, there is little doubt that it will become popular among a special group who have inherited that infinite patience from their ancestors.

There are collectors today who are searching for the old lace pillows and bobbins to *use*, not simply to display as has been the custom in the past. Some still want them just as decorative objects or because they are in some way related to their needlework collection. Out there somewhere in trunks, boxes, and old sewing baskets are yards and yards of old lace, lace collars, berthas, hats, fans, and parasols just waiting for the right collector to display them as is or recycle them into a stunning modern blouse or dress.

CHAPTER 15
The Evolution of Netting

Netting for household linens and clothing evolved, it seems, from the fisherman's net made of cords. The same type of netting is still used for both fishing and for the entrance to old wooden lobster traps. This change from fishing nets to fine netting didn't come all at once, but by evolution.

Some of the fishermen were also farmers or had farmers in their families. Since fencing other than stone fences was practically unknown many years ago, they began using netting around their gardens to keep animals and their own poultry out. Containers made of netting were used to harvest the gardens and some of the crops. They also found that a finer netting could be used to protect the fruit trees from attacks by birds. Their wives found that they could pen in the poultry with netting. They also used netting to store fruits and vegetables for winter.

Fisherman's netting has been in use for so long that it would be impossible to trace its origin. But it is believed by some researchers that netting for clothing and household linens was introduced into Europe by people returning from the Orient around the twelfth century. The use of embroidery on handmade netting is believed to have begun around the fourteenth century.

Sometime before the fourteenth century someone discovered that by using smaller cord or thread and smaller tools, netting could be made much finer and then could be made into garments. They also found that by embroidering designs on it with gold and silver threads, it could be made into gorgeous gar-

ments popular among royalty and the very rich.

As with all types of needlework, few if any records were kept of the early years. It was not until around 1825 to 1850 that any instructions were published or any records kept. In one of the earliest needlework books found so far, Mrs. Pullan's *The Lady's Manual of Fancy Work*, there are several pages devoted to the various types of hand netting being done at that time. Types listed were square, round, Grecian, spotted diamond, large diamond, diamond, and leaf. Each created a different design in the netting.

She gave instructions for netting with beads: "Instead of a netting needle, use an ordinary darner, of such size that the beads can pass over it. Thread as many beads as you wish to put on one stitch, then net as usual. Thread on more beads and do the next." According to these instructions the beads would have been put on or in the netting as it was made, not sewn on later.

Contrary to public opinion, darned and embroidered netting are not the same thing. In darned netting, threads are worked into the netting to form a geometric design. Embroidered netting is exactly what the name implies—the embroidery is done on the netting.

Both types became much more popular after the machine-made versions became available. Making netting by hand was a long and rather tedious chore, but when one could go to the store and buy pieces like baby caps, fancy scarves to wear with dresses or blouses, and

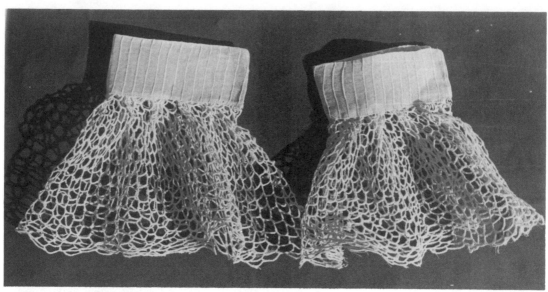

Cuffs with wide netted borders.

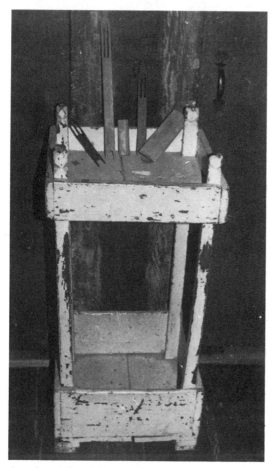

Stand used for making and mending larger netting.

Wedding handkerchief with hemstitching and netted edging.

embroidered lace netting by the yard, much more was used.

From the mid-1800s through the 1900s it was not unusual for one type of needlework to be known by several different names. Flanders lace is an example. According to Mrs. Pullan, Flanders lace, also known as darned or ecclesiastical lace, was a variety of darned netting that

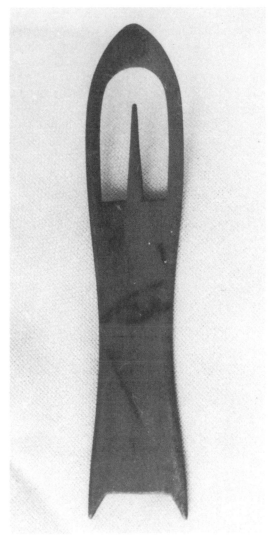

Style of netting needle different from the standard long slender version.

Front of blouse made with embroidered netting fagotted together.

formerly had been used to make ecclesiastical items. The netting always had to be square or oblong and the pattern or design marked on point paper. It then was darned so that every square to be filled in had four of the darning threads crossing it, two in each direction. Mrs. Pullan went on to say that she thought it was more difficult to acquire skill in making Flanders lace than any other type of fancy work because the worker never crossed two threads at a time and the whole must appear woven, with one thread above and one below. She didn't think it could be taught with written instructions.

The women of New England seemed to make more netting than those in other areas, possibly due to their proximity to the coast and the work of fishermen. It is still possible to find numerous articles either in darned netting or with borders of handmade netting. Especially desirable is the so-called wedding handkerchief, the one the bride carries during the ceremony. Handkerchiefs were an important part of the woman's costume a century or so ago, so it was only natural she would want a fancy, handmade one for her wedding. One lady who remembers them well says the wedding handkerchief usually was made by the bride's best friend, and the choicest ones had a drawn work design just above the handmade netted edging.

Apparently because the gauges can come in so many different sizes, it seems there are more tools associated with netting than with most other types of needlework. Although hoops or a frame were needed with embroidery, gauges and netting needles in assorted sizes were used in netting. But the most unusual item associated with netting is the stirrup, described by Mrs. Pullan as "a strip of embroidered canvas, an inch wide and five or six inches long, lined with ribbon, of which about a yard and a quarter is left, forming a long loop from one end of the canvas to the other. This is worn on the foot, the foundation of the netting being attached to the ribbon, which ought to be long enough to come within a pleasant range of sight. But, though not so neat and pretty, a fine cord passed around the foot answers all the purpose; and still better is a small cushion screwed to the edge of the table."

CHAPTER 16
New Uses for Antique Linens, Lace, and Needlework

Today there are probably less than one hundred housewives who still use the tidy or antimacassar as grandmother did—on the backs and arms of chairs. A few more still use centerpieces as they were originally intended, but the number is growing who realize old embroidered or crocheted tablecloths add a touch of elegance to meals like nothing else can.

Old crocheted bedspreads still add a touch of class to antique beds. A new use also has been found for open and lacy crocheted bedspreads and tablecloths—as canopy covers on both old and new beds.

Only a few people may be using the old needlework pieces as they originally were intended (the number has grown rapidly during the past two or three years), but there is a whole new generation recycling the old pieces and finding modern uses for otherwise antique castoffs. They are using many of the pieces just as they find them, but in a different way. A good example is the new use found for tidies or other seemingly useless pieces of crochet. One or more of the pieces—depending on the size of both the crochet and the pillow—are being put on throw pillows to make a delightful and interesting addition to any room. They even have been used to save a favorite pillow that met with an accident. The damaged place can be mended and then covered with a piece of closely done crochet. The idea is so simple that anyone who can use a needle and thread can make a new pillow in an hour or so.

Once the decision has been made and the pieces assembled, the crochet is placed on the top of the pillow, pinned in place, and then whipped on to hold it. This is one time the creator can let her imagination run wild. The pillow top can be completely covered with the crochet, or she might just want to use a small piece in the center. It was thought that the brighter the background, the prettier the pillow, but it was found that a brown pillow with ecru crochet was most attractive in a room done in greens and orange.

Doll dress with recycled braid and trim.

177

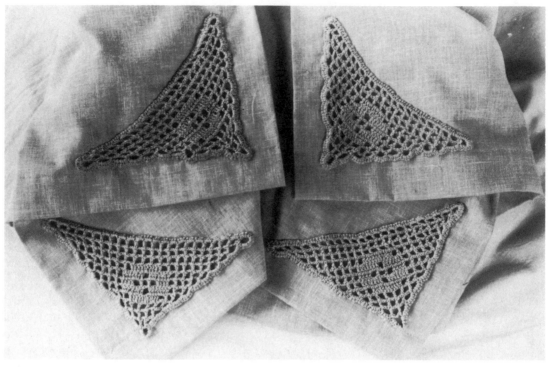

Odd-shaped, crocheted pieces were used on the corners of this tablecloth.

The same idea applies to monograms found on damaged linens. Cut out the monogram and put it on a pillow. Follow the same rules for application, except in this case the raw edges of the fabric must be turned under before it is whipped into place.

While searching for these pieces, don't pass up other pieces—regardless of size or shape—if the price if right. Small oblong pieces of crochet lined with various pieces of fabric from the scrap bag make good bags or purses. The small clutch bag shown in the illustrations was made by first lining the oblong piece of crochet with blue brocade left over from an evening dress. The lining was whipped on much like putting the crochet on a pillow, except this was easier. Then the sides were sewn together and an old button (for fastening) was attached. It makes a pretty and unique clutch bag for a teenager's summer dance.

The same idea can be used with a larger piece of crochet to make a shoulder bag. To make a bag for everyday use, line it with denim. Make it exactly like the clutch bag, but add a shoulder strap. The strap can be made with a long strip of crochet, and there are many pieces like that to be found. To strengthen the strap, the crochet can be doubled and lined with denim.

Framing pieces of needlework is as popular as making lamps out of old and otherwise useless pieces. The theory is, if you can't find a use for it, frame it. This is especially true for unusual pieces that are so intricate and pretty there is no other way to enjoy them. This is the perfect solution for enjoying crocheted gloves and collars. Crocheted purses are also easy to frame and are very attractive.

Handkerchiefs with tatted, crocheted, and knitted borders can be found today at reasonable prices considering all the work that was required to make them. But using handkerchiefs for the purpose for which they were made is about as out-of-date as the Wright brother's plane. Although they may have lost some of their popularity as handkerchiefs, they have become accepted for use in other ways. For instance, they are being used now to make big gathered skirts reminis-

French laid monogram from damaged piece was added to this pillow.

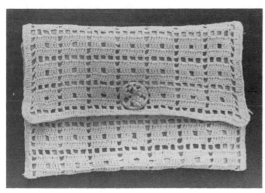

Clutch bag made from an odd piece of crochet.

bedspreads. Some of the spreads are lined, others are not.

Whenever working with recycled old needlework (and this is not a suggestion that good pieces be cut up simply for experimentation) there always will be some small pieces that

cent of the 1950s. The handkerchiefs are turned to form diamonds rather than being used square, although one very pretty skirt has been seen made with the handkerchiefs square. Generally, the big floral ones are used to make the skirts, and they also are being used to make

Square of lace adds to the beauty of a denim knitted bag.

Black beading matted on white velvet and framed.

Late paperweight with lace added.

seem to have no further use. Never throw them away. An idea will come along where they can be used.

Old inexpensive glass paperweights from the war years and earlier, found in every resort town with pictures of the local attractions glued underneath, are given new life when the picture is replaced with a bit of lace. They were made in both round and oblong shapes and now can be found priced around $1 each. If the original picture has not been removed, it can be soaked off in a few minutes. When it is clean and dry, turn the paperweight upside down, place a bit of lace in the recessed section, and glue felt over the back.

It is not unusual to find tatting and crocheted edgings in long lengths. Oftentimes these pieces are so twisted and dirty that it is impossible to see the beauty until it is washed. These lengths of handmade edging are very attractive when sewed on the edge of old monogrammed pillowcases, the same ones that are found in the stacks of linens. The edging is also attractive on new pillowcases. This edging can be used on the necks, sleeves, and around the yokes of modern dresses and blouses.

Another conversion of old needlework that requires absolutely no skill yet makes a stunning item is the old crocheted tassel, the shade pull. Since old window shade pulls are about as purposeless as the tidy, the tassels can be found now and then in shops specializing in linens and lace. All that is necessary once the tassel has been washed is to tie a key, possibly the utility room key, on the end and hang it on the key rack. It is not only very attractive, but it also is easy to find with the long tassel.

All the needlework books and magazines issued around the turn of the century had numerous illustrations and even more instructions for making yokes for nightgowns, chemises, and corset covers. Today those same yokes can be used for nightgowns or for summer blouses.

It is interesting to see how many pieces of unfinished crochet about one to three inches wide and from six to eighteen inches long can be found in any box of old linens. Whether they were made for a specific purpose, started as a project that was later abandoned, or were simply practice pieces is unknown. They fit into our modern world beautifully. With an old cameo pin or any type of old-fashioned pin, the crocheted strips can be made into exquisite chokers. Worn with an old-fashioned dress, they are absolutely adorable. A small piece of elastic fastened to either end of some of these crocheted pieces makes an excellent headband or bandeau.

In a room where there is only one window, old dresser scarves—especially the kind with medallions of filet crochet—make excel-

Crocheted piece makes choker when cameo pin is added.

Pincushions made by using crocheted doilies over craft Styrofoam and jar ring bases.

lent valances for use with old lace curtains. It is not necessary to cut or damage the scarf in any way. All that is necessary is a wide hem on the back, then a second row of machine stitching through that to form a header. When the valance is no longer needed, the hem can be easily ripped out and the old scarf reverts to its original use.

If the grandmothers of America never are given credit for anything else, they should be applauded for not only keeping their homes immaculate, but also for serving good food correctly—on finely done linens. At that time fashion decreed there should be doilies for everything from the tumbler to the violet bowl. Those housewives worked their fingers to the bone to produce set after set of embroidered or crocheted doilies. From all indications today they made an abundance, which can be found stacked in shops that specialize in linens. There aren't many uses today for the small crocheted ones unless they can be converted to pincushions or used on doll furniture or as Christmas tree ornaments.

One of the best ways to make a pincushion is to begin with the old craft pincushion that was popular a few decades ago. They were made by covering one half of a good-sized styrofoam ball with some type fabric like velvet and then inserting the ball into a metal fruit jar ring. Cover the ring with some type of braid. These small doilies or pieces left over from a crocheted bedspread or tablecloth work well when they are simply draped over the top of one of those pincushions and the center of each scallop is pinned to the base. This can be done with regular dressmaker's pins, the kind with small heads so they will not show later.

Another use for these small doilies or medallions is to lace them together with ribbon. When unlaced, they become doilies or medallions again. Before the sides are completely closed, the inner compartment is filled with potpourri, or cotton saturated with the owner's favorite perfume. Victorian ladies used cotton more than potpourri. A long length of ribbon can be left to hang on dress hangers while only a bow is necessary for the sachets to be used in drawers.

Quite often small bags or sewing baskets will be found filled with crocheted medallions, usually small ones, that were being made individually and later would be joined together to make a dresser scarf, centerpiece, tablecloth, or even a bedspread. Once in a while the partially finished piece will be found with them. In that case always use the loose pieces to complete the piece, provided there are enough. If there are only three or four dozen, they make wonderful decorations for a small Christmas tree, especially if a centerpiece made from the same design is used under the tree. Another great use for the loose medallions is as tablecloths for doll or miniature furniture.

Other items abundantly made by the Victorian ladies were towels and splashers; today there remains a bountiful supply. A few towels hanging in the bathroom is attractive, but most people prefer either paper towels or terry towels for everyday use, which leaves a lot of old towels. Many of those fancy monogrammed towels with crocheted or tatted borders are just waiting to be recycled. There may be others, but this one is easy to make. Convert the towel to a drawstring bag using only the material in the towel. The one used in the

Crocheted tumbler doilies were used to cover a satin ball for a Christmas tree decoration.

Small Christmas tree decorated with crocheted medallions and satin balls.

Miniature table and chairs with crocheted medallion used as a tablecloth.

illustration was a white towel with red borders down either side and red and white tatting on either end with a wider row of red and white tatting insertion. Enough fabric was cut from the center to make the drawstrings, but caution was used to cut them so that the red strips would be on the ends of the strings. The two pieces of towel were then sewed together across the bottom and up either side. The drawstrings were laced through the tatting insertion, knots were tied in the ends, and the bag was ready to use.

Various lengths of handmade lace that seem to have no other use can be used inside an antique frame. After the photo is placed on the mat, a piece of lace is arranged along the edge on all four sides, and the mat and photo returned to the frame. This is especially attractive when used with baby pictures.

As the popularity of old needlework continues to grow, prices are growing with it,

which means that collectors are finding more and more uses for the damaged pieces. There was a time when only doll collectors wanted the damaged pieces to use in doll dressmaking. Now the makers of new furry rabbits are using

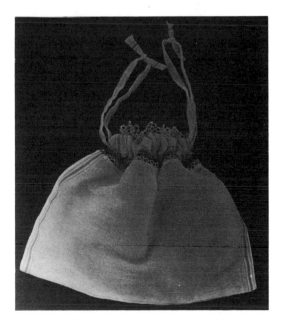

Drawstring bag made from a towel.

odds and ends of damaged embroidered pieces to line the rabbit's ears. Good portions salvaged from damaged pieces can be used to make lamp shades. Pieces from old woven coverlets, both the solid white and those done in colors, also can be used to make lamp shades. Larger pieces from both the coverlets and squares from damaged old quilts can be used to make throw pillows.

Since people who still use fabric napkins are few, and complete sets of napkins not as easy to find as they once were, some collectors are making beautiful throw pillows using the heavily embroidered napkins. They are very pretty when used on a bed with an old white woven or crocheted bedspread.

This author comes from a "waste not, want not" family, and remembers well how the mothers, aunts, and grandmothers utilized needlework until there was nothing left. In the beginning the damaged pieces were patched with small pieces of fabric sewn very carefully and expertly under and around the hole. When the piece was absolutely passed salvaging, it was cut up and the small pieces made into doll clothes for the children. Larger pieces, like dresser scarves and small tablecloths, were recycled into bedspreads and pillowcases for my doll bed or carriage.

CHAPTER 17

Hints on Caring for Antique Linens and Lace

So much time and effort was expended on each piece of needlework that it behooves the new owner—whether it was the maker, someone who received the piece as a gift, or someone who purchased it—to learn to care for it well. Accidents will happen, and for that reason grandmother discovered, probably by trial and error methods, various and sundry ways to renew pieces of needlework to their original beauty. Magazines in those days often carried "hints" on how to remove stains, and some of the magazines—especially those devoted entirely to needlework—gave explicit directions for laundering needlework.

We do not recommend all of these methods because some will work on one type of material but will not work on another. The old linens we find today already are worn from use and some are beginning to dry-rot from being stored in the wrong places for too long. Some of them were packed away filled with starch, which is damaging to the fabric. For that reason each person has to make her own decision on how to clean and restore the old linens she has found. The following hints and suggestions have been gathered from old magazines, diaries, and word-of-mouth home remedies. They are offered merely as ideas that worked in another day on new materials and fabrics, but are *not recommended for old linens unless the owner is willing to take a chance.*

It has been found that this new method will work on old linens provided the fabric is still good and the yellowing was caused by the piece being packed in an exposed position over a long period of time. We learned by trial and error that most of the yellowing and dirt accu-mulation from storing could be removed by simply soaking the linens overnight in a bath-tub full of cold water. The next day a few pieces at a time are removed to the sink where they are washed in warm water and mild soap with as little rubbing or squeezing as possible. It also has been found that modern inventions will work on old linens. Sometimes the yellow age stains are stubborn and will not wash out with soaking and light washing. In that case we have used a few drops of Woolite. This is not guar-anteed to work in every case as some of the fabric, already old and worn, will begin to tear apart from too much handling while it is wet. Therefore, it is imperative that each piece be examined carefully before any type of cleaning is begun to ascertain whether or not it will withstand the process.

The commonly accepted way to wash new embroidered linens (made with cotton or linen thread), is to use warm water, but "not quite as warm as the hand could bear." The soap always should be mild, and most dedicated workers at that time specified the use of Ivory soap. One was warned against rubbing and twisting the linens any more than was absolutely necessary to remove the dirt, in fact they stressed the point that all linens should be washed as quickly as possible by squeezing the suds back and forth through the fabric. It was suggested that water from the spring was preferable to well water or any other type of water. After the linens were washed they were rinsed twice in "clear, soft water, then placed between two linen towels to dry." One was cautioned not to roll up the linens in the towels, fold them, or expose them to the sun. Later linens would be laid on the grass so the sun could "bleach" them snowy white, but this usually was done to the damask pieces without embroidery.

Linens embroidered with silk thread were treated a bit differently when they were laundered. It was suggested that they never be put in with the regular wash, but should be washed separately in an "eathern bowl." The method was about the same as for washing other pieces except that fairly hot water was used and it was suggested that the embroidered pieces be rolled up in drying towels. The silk threads had to be perfectly dry before ironing because "a hot iron placed upon embroideries in which silk is wet will produce a steam which will take the life from the silk and ruin the embroidery." If the fabric center became too dry to iron smooth, a damp cloth was placed over it.

Grandmother took as much pride in the care of her linens as she did in the execution of them, and she had her own special way of ironing embroidered linens. Once they were dry, they were first ironed like any other piece and then sorted into two piles. One pile consisted of the everyday linens including the embroidered pillowcases, tablecloths, doilies, and centerpieces (pieces that were getting older, weren't elaborately done, and were used every day by the family). The other stack was made up of the exquisitely done linens that required so much work and only were used on Sunday and when guests were coming.

Now the fine ironing began. First, the everyday pieces were ironed again, once on the top, and then turned and ironed with a moderately hot iron on the wrong side to make the embroidery stand out more clearly. The best pieces got the royal treatment. The "cloths" that were saved especially for ironing the best linens were brought from the pantry. A piece of heavy flannel was put on top of the already well-padded ironing board. The embroidered piece was laid on the flannel with the embroidered side down. On top of this was placed a soft dry white cloth and then a wet one. Finally, a dry white cloth was placed over the other two, and it was time to start ironing. Still using a moderately hot iron, the work began in the center with the ironer always working toward the outside. With frequent checks she was able to see when the embroidery reached

the perfect stage. Perfection in this case meant the embroidery looked like it had been laid on the fabric rather than sewed through it.

Despite grandmother's constant vigil, accidents did occur. Tea or coffee was spilled on the linens. To remove these stains she simply placed the stained portion of the cloth over a bowl and poured boiling water through it. This method worked best on fresh stains.

As everyone knows, spilling the juice of a fresh peach on fabric is not only ugly and brown, but it also is almost impossible to remove. The old method was to soak colored fabric in milk for forty-eight hours. On white tablecloths a little lemon juice and salt were rubbed on the stain and then it was soaked.

One of the hazards affecting linens nearly a century ago was iron rust. To remove it muratic acid was applied to the spot and it was rubbed until the stain disappeared. The linens were then thoroughly rinsed several times, with the first rinse water containing a small amount of ammonia to counteract the acid.

To remove gravy grease spots from tablecloths, grandmother moistened the spot with ammonia water, laid a piece of blotting paper over it, and ironed it dry. If the grease was extremely heavy, the process might have to be repeated several times.

Oftentimes kitchen curtains—and in a few cases where it was important that everything match—kitchen towels, were made of pretty gingham. Aprons, often lavishly embroidered, also were made of gingham. In those days fabrics had a tendency to fade regardless of the type or the cost. To prevent fading from the first washing to the last, old-timers added a teaspooon of turpentine to one gallon of luke-warm water and soaked the new ginghams for an hour. When the soaking was completed, they were washed like the other clothing and linens, rinsed thoroughly, and hung in the shade to dry.

For some unknown reason needleworkers of a century or so ago had persistent problems with their linens mildewing. One of the many methods prescribed for the removal of mildew specified that the linen be wet with soft water and rubbed well with a mild soap and white powdered chalk. It then was placed flat on the grass in very hot sunshine and watched carefully so that it could be kept damp. The same process was repeated until the mildew was gone (usually in three or four days).

Nearly a century ago money was scarce in most rural households, making it difficult for the housewife to obtain linens stamped ready for embroidery. Of course the iron-on designs were less expensive, but there were times when some people could not even afford them. In some cases the worker was unable to find a design that she felt merited the work involved. So it was not unusual for the more-talented workers to either sketch a design on the fabric or copy one from a neighbor's linens. For the less talented a way other than sketching had to be devised. The origin of this method is unknown, but it did work. The embroidered piece to be copied was laid on a table or any other hard, smooth surface. The fabric for the new piece was laid directly over the first piece and pinned in place. Then one of the ladies simply took a snuff box with a smooth surface on the lid, rubbed it over her hair, and then rubbed it across a portion of the work. This process was repreated until the entire design was transferred from the old to the new.

Quite often now old linens—especially small tablecloths and napkins—will be found monogrammed and with the edges fringed rather than hemmed. Occasionally pieces will be found with a second piece of fabric sewn on the edge and fringed. This is not a later addition. The early workers preferred thick, luxurious fringe, but most fabrics will not make it with one thickness. Therefore, they added a small strip, fringed both, and it looked like one thickness. These strips usually were added at the edge of the hemstitching or where the row of stitching marks the end of the fringing. After numerous washings the fringe has a tendency to mat or twist together. This matted fringe can be made to look like new by brushing it with a stiff clothes brush.

Now that old lace is experiencing such a revival or recycling, it is imperative that it be cleaned properly before use. Grandmother had a special method for washing lace. First she sewed the cut-off leg of a soft, firm, heavy cotton stocking tightly over an old wine bottle. Then she wound pieces of soiled lace, sometimes small lace collars, and edging smoothly around the covered bottle. With a whipping stitch she sewed the laces to the stocking, being careful to catch each loop. The bottle was then swished up and down in a pail of warm, soapy water. On stubborn stains she used a soft sponge to work back and forth across the spot. The laces were rinsed in the same fashion using bucket after bucket of fresh water until all traces of suds were gone. A weak solution of gum arabic was applied, and the bottle was put in the sun so the laces could dry. Since it was felt that ironing damaged fine laces, the method used then was to carefully remove the laces once they were completely dry and then place them between the white pages of a heavy book. If one preferred ironing to the book-pressing method, the lace was placed in several folds of muslin and then ironed.

If you are ever lucky enough to find some of the old lace made with gold and silver threads, you might want to try the following rememdy for removing tarnish. If the gold is worn away it cannot be restored without regilting if that is still possible today. Considering the price of gold, it would cost a great amount of money if it *was* possible. But if it is simply tarnished, warm a small quantity of wine and apply it to the lace with the softest (fine sable is recommended) brush available. It was suggested that the warm wine be rubbed gently into every area of the lace, brushing repeatedly until the lace resumes its natural luster.

To keep a new piece of tatting fresh and in good shape, use a special pressing process. Place the piece between two cloths before pressing. The one on the bottom is thick and soft while the one on top should be wrung out of cold starch. Ironing continues until the top cloth is completely dry.

The old suggestion on roll hemming should be especially helpful now that old lace is being used in so many ways. If you want the roll to be very fine when rolling and whipping on lace, baste the lace about one-eighth of an inch from the edge of the fabric on the right side. As the whipping begins, the material rolls into a small, neat hem as the work progresses. The basting is removed when the work is completed.

Bibliography

BOOKS

Baker, Muriel L. *The ABCs of Canvas Embroidery*. Sturbridge, Mass.: Old Sturbridge Booklet Series, 1968.

———. *The XYZs of Canvas Embroidery*. Sturbridge, Mass.: Old Sturbridge Booklet Series, 1971.

Caplin, Jessie F. *The Lace Book*. New York: MacMillan Publishing Co., 1932.

Caulfield, Sophia, Anne Frances, and Blanche C. Saward. *The Dictionary of Needlework*. 1882. Reprint. New York: Arno Press, 1972.

Clabburn, Pamela. *Samplers*. London, England: Shire Publications, Ltd., 1977.

Close, Eunice. *Lace Making*. London, England: John Gifford, Ltd., 1951.

Coats and Clark, Inc. *J. and P. Coats 100 Embroidery Stitches*. Jacksonville, Fla.: Coats and Clark, Inc., 1979.

Curry, David Park. *Stitches in Time*. Lawrence, Ks.: University of Kansas Museum of Art, 1975.

deDillmont, Therese. *Masterpieces of Irish Crochet Lace*. Reprint. Mineola, N.Y.: Dover Publications, Inc., 1986.

Denny, Grace Goldena. *Fabrics and How to Know Them*. Philadelphia: J. B. Lippincott Co., 1923.

Dolan, Maryanne. *Old Lace and Linens*. Florence, Ala.: Books Americana, 1989.

Earle, Alice Morse. *Customs and Fashions in Old New England*. New York: Charles Scribners' Sons, 1893.

Elliot, Maud Howe. *Arts and Handicrafts and Women's Building*, Chicago World's Columbian Exposition, 1893. New York: Goupil and Co., 1893.

Feldman, Annette. *Handmade Lace and Patterns*. New York: Harper and Row, Publishers Inc., 1975.

Fitch, Mary. *Filet Crochet with Instructions*. Brookline, Mass.: Self-published, 1913.

Gordon, Beverly. *Shaker Textile Arts*. Hanover, N.H.: University Press of New England, 1980.

Groves, Sylvia. *The History of Needlework Tools and Accessories*. New York: Arco Publishing Co., 1973.

Hall, Carrie A. and Rose G. Kretsinger. *The Romance of the Patchwork Quilt in America*. New York: Bonanza Books, 1935.

Hapgood. *School Needlework*, teacher's ed. Needham, Mass.: Ginn and Co., 1908.

Haraszty, Eszter, and Bruce David Colen. *Needlepainting: A Garden of Stitches*. New York: Liveright, 1974.

Hedlund, Catherine A. *A Primer of New England Crewel Embroidery*. Sturbridge, Mass.: Old Sturbridge, Inc., 1963.

Hopewell, Jeffrey. *Pillow Lace and Bobbins*. London, England: Shire Publications, Ltd., 1975.

Jackson, F. Nevill. *Old Handmade Lace.* Mineola, N.Y.: Dover Publications, Ltd., 1987. A combination of five 1900 books.

Johnson, Eleanor. *Needlework Tools.* London, England: Shire Publications, Ltd., 1978.

Kellogg, Charlotte. *Bobbins of Belgium.* Ramsey, N.J.: Funk and Wagnalls, 1920.

Nicholls, Elgiva. *Tatting Technique and History.* London, England: Longacre Press, Ltd., 1962.

Palliser, Bury. *History of Lace.* 1911. Reprint. Mineola. N.Y.: Dover Publications, Inc., 1984.

Polkinghorne, R. K. and M. I. R. *The Art of Needlecraft.* London, England: Associated Newspapers, Ltd., n.d.

Preston, Doris Campbell. *Needle-Made Laces and Net Embroideries.* Reprint. Mineola, N.Y.: Dover Publications, Inc., 1984.

Pullan. *The Lady's Manual of Fancy Work.* New York: Dick and Fitzgerald, 1858.

Silk Association of America. *The Romantic Story of Silk.* New York: Silk Association of America, 1926.

Snook, Barbara. *English Historical Embroidery.* London, England: B. T. Batsford, Ltd., 1960.

Swain, Margaret. *Ayshire and Other White Work.* London, England: Shire Publications, Ltd., 1982.

Traditional Hardanger Embroidery. 1924. Reprint. Mineola, N.Y.: Dover Publications, Inc., 1985.

Waller, Kathleen. *Introducing Filet Lace.* Westmidland, England: Self-published, 1987.

Whiting, Gertrude. *Old-Time Tools and Toys of Needlework.* 1928. Reprint. Mineola, N.Y.: Dover Publications, Inc., 1985.

PERIODICALS

Burroughs, Ada Maud. "Bead Work for the Amateur." *Home Needlework Magazine* (August/September 1911).

Coe, Eva Johnston. "American Samplers." *Country Life* (September 1928).

Cole, Alan S. "Old Embroidery." *Home Needlework Magazine* (October 1900).

Cooper, Eloise. "A Beautiful Wedding Gown in Decore Crochet." *Home Needlework Magazine* (July 1906).

"Embroidery Stitches." *Popular Needlework* (July/August 1976).

Harris, Elizabeth. "Suggestions for the Lace Maker." *Home Needlework Magazine* (August 1909).

———. "New Ideas in Lace." *Home Needlework Magazine* (April 1906).

"Lacemaking (Battenberg)." *McCall's Magazine* (August 1899).

"Ladies' Point Lace Bertha." *The Delinator* (January 1902).

Leechman, Douglas. "The Magic Dyes of Olden Days." *American Home* (April 1930).

Levetus, A. S. "The Revival of Lace Making in Hungary." *The International Studio* (November 1910).

Mayer, Christa C. "Two Centuries of Needle Lace." *Antiques Magazine* (February 1965).

Needlecraft Magazine. All issues from 1920 through 1930.

"New Designs in Crochet Lace and Insertions." *McCall's Magazine* (November 1899).

Peto, Florence. "Hand-made White Elegance." *Antiques Magazine* (March 1948).

Thomas, Kathryn V. "Basket of Flowers Design in Filet." *Home Arts Needlecraft* (June 1938).

Walbran, Gertrude M. "A Lesson in Irish Crochet." *Home Needlework Magazine* (August 1909).

Wilson, L. Barton. "Lesson in Embroidery." *Home Needlework Magazine* (January 1900).

———. "The Theory and Method of Embroidery." *Home Needlework Magazine* (January 1902).

Index

Price Guide for Antique Linens, Lace, and Needlework

So many factors are involved in pricing antiques and collectibles that it would be impossible to compile a price guide that would be accurate for every section of the country. In some areas the supply may be plentiful but the demand lacking, while in other areas the situation may be reversed. An important factor is condition. Even slightly damaged needlework will not command the price perfect items will, regardless of the supply or demand. Then there is the matter of quality workmanship as opposed to poor workmanship. Not all needleworkers did excellent work. Therefore, please use this as a guide, not as figures carved in stone.

Album, photo, embroidery	17–24
Altar cloth	
crochet	16–27
embroidery	15–24
Antimacassar set	
3-piece	
crochet, plain	16–23
embroidery, late	10–13
filet crochet, animals,	
houses, etc.	33–39
4-piece loveseat set	30–36
Apron	
early crochet trim	12–19
embroidery	6–10
late, crochet	9–15
Baby bib	
crochet	7–10
embroidery	5–9

Baby cap	
crochet	18–24
tatted	35–50
Baby carriage cover	
crochet	35–49
embroidery	24–36
knit	35–49
Baby carriage strap	
crochet	19–27
embroidery	14–17
Bags, embroidery	
corset	12–14
darning	5–9
gloves	8–12
gowns	10–14
handkerchiefs	9–13
shirt, man's or woman's	11–17
silverware, knives, forks,	
and spoons, each	7–9
table linens	9–15
ties, crochet or	
embroidery	12–19
Basket, crochet	10–15
Bedspreads	
crochet, early	175–275
crochet, late	150–225
embroidery, late	95–150
embroidery, wool-on-	
wool	350–500
knit	175–275
Belt, crochet	12–17
Birch bark box	
moosehair embroidery	200–250
porcupine quill	
embroidery	125–190

split porcupine quill embroidery	175–215
Bobbins, lace pillow	
beads	14–17
wood	7–9
Bodkins	
celluloid	9–14
ivory, fancy	75–85
silver plate	16–25
sterling	28–44
Book cover, crochet	25–39
Bookmark	
crochet	4–6
embroidery, perforated paper	9–11
tatted	10–15
Boudoir cap	
crochet	16–19
knit	19–21
tatted	25–35
Bread basket cover, embroidery	5–8
Bread tray cover	
crochet	12–15
embroidery	11–13
Bridge tablecloth or cover (with four matching napkins, the cost is 20% more.)	
Battenberg	80–90
crocheted corners and edging	19–36
cutwork	25–37
drawn work	26–39
embroidery	15–24
Calendar holder, embroidery	10–15
Carving cloth	
drawn work	16–22
embroidery	9–15
hemstitched, fringed	8–12
Centerpiece, round, small to medium (The large size costs 20% more.)	
Battenberg	17–25
crochet	7–13
cutwork	9–14
drawn work	10–19
embroidery, late, colored	5–9

embroidery, white-on-white	7–12
hairpin work	8–11
knit	7–10
tatting	9–14
Chair back, only, no arm covers	
crochet	10–15
knit	11–17
Chatelaine	
silver plate	125–165
sterling	200–250
sweetgrass, Indian-made	90–110
Clock shelf cloth	
crochet trim	9–12
drawn work	15–18
embroidery	6–10
Collar, dress	
crochet, plain	9–13
Irish lace crochet	17–20
Collar and cuff set	
crochet	18–20
Irish lace crochet	25–30
Cotton barrel for thread, wood	12–17
Coverlet, woven	150–300
Cozy	
embroidery, bread or rolls	9–15
embroidery, teapot	10–16
Crochet hook	
bone	9–11
ivory, fancy	29–37
metal, late	3–4
wood, handmade	9–13
Doily (Some were made of or decorated with all types of needlework. Battenberg, tatting and drawnwork will be approximately 10% higher.)	
bullion	4–6
bread and butter	6–8
bread tray	7–9
celery	6–8
creamer	8–10
cup	3–5
finger bowl	8–10

frappé	6–9	sterling	150–200
olive dish	10–13	Hooked rug	300–400
pickle dish	9–12	Jabot, lace	
rose bowl	11–15	fancy	18–25
7-piece lemonade set	20–32	plain	15–19
sugar	8–10	Key holder, crochet	6–8
tumbler	4–6	Lacemaker's lamp	175–350
Door hanging, filet crochet	17–30	Lace pillow	
Dress, lady's		American wooden	95–175
child's, embroidery, tucking, tatting	65–175	early velvet	35–75
combination lace and embroidery	125–300	Library table scarf or runner	
Dresser scarf or runner		Battenberg	105–155
Battenberg	65–125	crochet trim	18–35
crochet trim	22–46	cutwork	55–75
drawn work	25–49	drawn work	45–55
embroidery, cotton	16–26	embroidery	15–34
embroidery, silk on felt	27–38	knit trim	19–29
knit trim	23–39	tatted trim	22–32
tatted trim, insertion	24–45	Medicine glass cover	
Edging or lace, handmade, by the yard (Add 20% for wider edging.)		crochet	3–6
		embroidery	2–5
		Miser's purse, early, bead crochet	29–50
crochet	2–3	Napkins, set of 6	
hairpin work	4–5	crochet trim	9–20
knit	3–4	cutwork	12–18
tatting	3–5	damask, hemstitched border	8–12
Embroidery frame, old, wood	11–17	drawn work	15–25
Embroidery hoops		monogrammed	19–27
early wood	5–6	tatted trim	12–20
late metal	3–4	24-by-24-inch size	18–30
Emery balls or berries		Napkin rings, set of 6	
fabric covered	3–5	crochet	12–15
sterling top	15–17	monogrammed	15–18
Eyeglass case, embroidery, wool	10–13	tatted	15–20
Gloves, dress, pair		Needle cabinet, old store display	250–450
crochet, fancy	18–30	Needle case, birch bark, Indian-made	8–11
crochet, plain	12–19	Needle painting or silk embroidery, silk-on-silk, Estonia-made	65–98
knit	10–17		
Handkerchief			
crochet trim	2–5		
drawn work	4–7	Netting gauge, wood, all sizes	9–13
embroidery	2–4	Netting needle,	
tatted trim	4–8	bone, handmade	9–15
wedding	9–12	wood, handmade	10–17
Hemming or sewing bird, old		Netting stand, wood	250–300
silver plate	95–125		

Parasol or umbrella,		Quilts	
embroidered cover	115–155	appliqué	800–1100
Piano scarf or runner		appliqué, fancy	1000–3500
Battenberg	49–75	crazy, velvet	300–500
crochet trim	17–31	embroidered	500–750
cutwork	19–32	pieced, fancy	1000–2500
drawn work	22–30	pieced, plain	300–900
embroidery	13–18	Sachet, crochet	9–13
tatted trim and insertion	20–33	Sampler	
Picture frame, embroidery	22-30	early	500–900
Pillowcases, muslin or		late	150–200
percale, pair (Linen		motto	75–145
costs 20 to 30 percent		Scissors	
more.)		buttonhole	5–8
crocheted edging	18–27	embroidery	7–9
cutwork	20–29	sewing	6–9
drawn work	20–29	sterling handles	30–42
embroidery, color	15–19	stork handles	10–15
embroidery, white-on-		Scissor sheath, sweet grass,	
white	18–28	Indian-made	9–17
knit trim	16–23	Serving tray cover	
monogrammed	18–29	crochet trim	11–15
tatted trim	19–28	drawn work	13–19
Pillow top, throw		embroidery, red or	
Battenberg	25–35	white	10–18
China ribbon	15–19	Sewing basket	
drawn work	17–23	Indian-made	45–59
embroidery, Art Deco	10–14	Shaker, lined	255–325
embroidery, regular	7–11	Sewing or hemming bird,	
Pillow shams, pair		old	
crochet	27–35	plain	95–125
embroidery, turkey red	35–75	silver plate	150–200
embroidery, white	29–39	Sewing box, one-drawer,	
Pincushions		wood, pincushion top	85–105
beaded, Indian-made	35–75	Sewing kit or case	
crochet	15–20	celluloid tools	23–35
embroidery	17–25	silver plate tools	75–115
lace	20–25	sterling tools	125–175
sweetgrass, Indian-made,		Sewing disk, sweet grass,	
velvet top	23–35	Indian-made	95–125
woven poplar, Shaker-		Sewing stand	
made	75–95	ash splint	65–95
Platter or meat tray cloth,		Victorian	150–200
embroidery	19–25	wicker, old	200–250
Pot holder		Sewing table	
filet crochet	17–24	old, well-made	900–1300
plain crochet	7–9	Victorian, dropleaf	600–800
Purse		Shade pulls	
bead, early crochet	75–105	crochet	4–6
bead, late, Indian-made	65–95	tatted	5–8
crochet, regular	19–26		

Shawl			silver plate	18–23
crochet	35–50		sterling	35–44
tatted	100–125		turtle	45–60
Shuttle, tatting			Tea cart cover	
advertising	10–15		crochet trim	15–19
celluloid, other	9–15		drawn work	25–30
ivory, fancy	75–125		embroidery	14–18
Lydia E. Pinkham			Tea tablecloth	
advertising, celluloid	25–35		Battenberg	85–105
silver plate	19–33		crochet	65–78
sterling	95–120		cutwork	95–105
tortoiseshell	45–75		drawn work	80–100
Sideboard runner or three-			embroidery	63–85
piece set			French knot embroidery	59–75
Battenberg	50–75		net trim	48–65
crochet trim	15–24		tatted trim	50–64
cutwork	19–27		Thimble, old	
drawn work	25–35		advertising	5–6
embroidery, color or			brass	6–8
white	16–27		celluloid	4–5
knit trim	18–30		gold	95–150
tatted trim	21–36		silver plate	20–35
Skein winder, wood	39–54		sterling	49–63
Stiletto			Thimble holder, sweet	
bone	18–20		grass	12–15
celluloid	9–13		Thread cabinet, store	
ivory	29–38		display	
sterling handle	35–45		2-drawer	95–125
Splashers, large towels			4-drawer	200–250
crochet trim	17–23		6-drawer	400–500
drawn work	19–25		Thread waxer	
monogrammed, 3 letters	21–29		celluloid	10–15
Stockings, pair			silver plate	19–27
knit, fancy	75–95		sterling	45–56
knit, plain	43–55		Towel	
Tablecloth, medium size			crochet trim	8–12
(Large size is 20%			embroidery	7–15
more.)			monogrammed, 3 letters	11–19
Battenberg	150–200		tatted trim	9–17
crochet	125–175		Umbrella or parasol,	
cutwork	125–175		embroidery cover	115–150
drawn work	100–135		Vanity set, 3-piece	
embroidery, color, late	65–75		crochet	14–19
embroidery, white-on-			embroidery	10–17
white	85–95		knit or tatted trim	11–19
tatted trim	75–85		Veil case	
Tape measure			embroidery, small	6–8
advertising	8–10		embroidery, large	8–10

About the Author

The old custom of a young girl spending so many hours each day doing her "daily stint" at needlework began early for the author. She was only five years old when her great grandmother, convinced that "Idle hands were the devil's workshop," began teaching her to do cross-stitch. She labored over those simple stitches for a year or longer because her grandmother was equally convinced that "Anything worth doing at all, was worth doing well." Grandma Strickland, who ruled her home and family with old adages, also said, "Practice makes perfect," and apparently she was right as the author soon mastered the perfect cross-stitch.

Later the author was taught other types of needlework, but her favorite always has been embroidery. She still treasures old needlework, especially the white on white with heavy embroidery and mixed designs. Perhaps the reason for that is the fact she knows how many hours were spent making the millions of tedious stitches—and she also knows needlework is probably one of the last entirely handmade things we will ever have.